GOD MAKES MY LITTLE TAIL *Wiggle*

LESSONS OF LOVE, LIFE, AND SEEING
THROUGH THE EYES OF THE DIVINE, TAUGHT
BY A DOG NAMED CODY

BOB & CODY WOLFF

GOD MAKES
MY LITTLE TAIL
Wiggle

LESSONS OF LOVE, LIFE, AND SEEING THROUGH THE EYES
OF THE DIVINE, TAUGHT BY A DOG NAMED CODY

BOB & CODY WOLFF

Published by
Tail Wiggle, LLC
10400 Overland Road, Suite 143
Boise, Idaho, USA 83709

Book Information:
www.CodyandBob.com
Cody & Bob ™
Tail Wiggle ™
Facebook: /codyandbobinspires
Instagram: @codyandbob

Library of Congress: 2018913144

Hardcover Print ISBN: 978-1-949653-58-8
Paperback Print ISBN: 978-1-949653-88-5
eBook ISBN: 978-1-949653-16-8
Audio Book ISBN: 978-1-949653-14-4

Inspirations

6

7

8

FOLLOWING THE INSPIRATION WITHIN

9

GOING FROM WHERE YOU ARE TO ANYWHERE YOU WANT TO BE

10

YOU ARE AMAZING, AND YOUR LIFE IS ABOUT TO BECOME EXTRAORDINARY   **261**

Introduction

I was just eight weeks old and weighed only a few pounds, and he could easily hold me in the palm of his hand.

When his green eyes looked into my sky blue eyes for the very first time, something deep inside of us was awakened.

Awakened in ways unlike anything we had ever known before.

He *knew* I would be his and I *knew* he would be mine.

It took only seconds, but those seconds would become a lifetime.

It was love at first sight, and instantly we both *knew* it was right.

I didn't find Bob.

Bob found me.

And God created *us* to find each other.

For the rest of my life, we would be together and inseparable.

I wasn't a puppy anymore.

We are *Bob & Cody* and we proudly let the world know it every moment we can.

We are one soul—a boy and his best friend—that lives, breathes, and moves in perfect harmony.

All of it choreographed like a beautiful symphony and dance we know will never end by the Master of All Creation.

God.

What we did not and could not know was how much having each other has forever changed us.

We are best friends living, laughing, and loving life together.

The lessons we learn about ourselves, about love, and about this life are a gift from the Divine.

With each new day that dawns, we realize even more, how those lessons have become life's priceless experiences that cannot and will not be traded for all the money and treasures in the world.

Each and every day, Bob and I show each other that the bond between the two of us and the animals we all love is the closest thing on Earth many of us will ever experience to knowing the unconditional love of God.

The love Bob inspires me to feel for him, and him for me, opens a pathway unlike any other to inspiration from the Divine.

And it does so in ways we never dreamed possible.

I am a dog.

Some call us their angel.

And not all of us angels have wings.

I am God's purity and love that came to this earth all wrapped up with big green eyes, floppy ears, four paws and a little tail.

I am your non-resistant, let-your-guard-down, open and flowing channel and direct pipeline to the Divine.

To that you call God or the Universe.

You will never meet one of us and not have your life touched in some way.

We are angels always looking for someone to help and to make their life happier and better.

We know things you don't, and we are here to remind you of the things you do.

As a dog, I never look forward or backward to some forgotten past or imagined future.

My pure animal love only knows one thing...

To be always present and always here in the moment, living and loving in each of those moments with every fiber of my being.

Yes, I'm a dog. And all us dogs live and give with everything we are in *this moment* and in all the moments to come.

You humans make your lives so difficult and so needlessly unhappy.

You do something we dogs can never do.

You wait for that someday when you'll *finally* start living and loving your life.

We do it every day.

It's now time for you to do it too.

When you have a dog, meet a dog, or love a dog, something happens most of you never realize.

Once you are in our lives, we will always be forever in yours.

A dog will touch your heart like nothing else and no one else can.

We'll make you laugh.

We'll make you sigh.

And when it's time for us to leave our bodies...

We'll make you cry.

We are your angels while we're here, wiggling our tail for you to see.

And we will always be your angels when it's time for us to leave this earth and be in the place where you can't see us.

For now.

We are always with you.

And if you'll let yourself, you'll feel our presence right here and right now and right where you are.

If you have ever met a dog or loved a dog, something is about to happen to your life that will change your life.

The help you've always wanted is about to come to you from a friend you never expected.

A dog.

What you call God or the Universe sends us to be with you, to guide you, to remind you and to inspire you to live the life you are being called to and to become who and what we know you can be.

And now I am about to tell you how.

All because you met and loved a dog.

It makes my little tail wiggle when I think of all the things Bob and I have taught each other.

We still do.

And always will.

Now.

And forever.

With our best wishes and love,
Bob & Cody

1

A FRESH WAY
OF THINKING FOR A NEW
WAY OF LIVING

> ## *I came into this life being happy, so what happened along the way?"*

You were such a happy kid.

You loved to play.

You loved to giggle and laugh.

You loved to explore.

You loved being curious and your curiosity knew no limits.

Then you began listening and watching those around you.

Those whose love and attention you desired.

And slowly... you became one of *them*.

And the more you did, the less *you* let yourself be.

You were taught conformity is a good thing and to be a good person, you need to be like *every other* person.

As you did, you began feeling unhappy.

You began feeling empty.

You began feeling you were playing a part that's not a part of you.

The years have passed and you've become quite good at being someone you're not.

And none of it makes you one bit happy.

I have a message for you...

It's time for the charade to end.

Dogs can never be something they're not.

We are dogs and dogs only know how to be who we are.

I never need a photo to look back on to remember how I was, because I've always been and will always be who God created me to be.

I never lost the purity and innocence and love that's God inside of me walking, barking, tail wiggling, and always excited.

That's all I know and that's all I live.

And so can you.

It's time for you to get back to being the original that God created *you* to be.

Go find an old photo of you as kid.

Find the one that when you see it, you instantly feel *"That's who I was."*

Put that photo in your closet or someplace you can see it all throughout the day.

And then pick it up and look at it. Not just once.

Pick it up and look at it *many* times during the day because holding that photo and looking at it is about to do something to you…

Remind you this is still who you are.

The real you has never changed.

The happy you has never changed.

The dreaming and playing you has never changed.

The *you* you see in the photo makes you feel the way you do because that's *who* God created you to be.

The *you* you see in the photo is the *you* who wants to come out and be *you* once again.

You came into this world being happy.

Let God show you how once again.

Dear God,

You created me to be happy and to love this life. I'm so grateful for every moment and every day of it. Thank you. Help me to get back to being who I truly am. I let go of anything that keeps me from being the happy, joyful, playful, loving-my-life child of yours that I am. Thank you for speaking to me, in the ways I know it comes from you, to do your will, to dream my dreams, and to let your divine perfect guidance fill me with peace, power, presence and direction to every dream that is in divine perfect harmony with your plan for my life. I love you God. Thank you. Yes… Amen.

♥

Only happy thoughts come from God"

In your world of people, it's been said, "Who needs enemies when the biggest one you'll ever face is within you?"

Have you ever wondered why you are so demanding on yourself?

Bob did, until I taught him a lesson on being happy.

God created me to think only happy thoughts.

I know nothing of being fearful, resentful, guilty, regretful, worrisome, or insecure, or wondering how I'm going to be cared for.

I never go to a grocery store to buy my favorite dog foods and treats, and yet I never miss a meal or go hungry.

I've never cleaned my water bowl or filled it with fresh cool water many times during the day, yet I *always* know I have delicious water that will never run out.

Think about this: God made all the creatures on this earth and always takes perfect care of them.

You are made in God's image, so just think how important it is to the one who made you to always take perfect care of you.

Whenever those unhappy thoughts come for a visit and want you to keep thinking about them, tell yourself, *"I like thinking about positive happy things"* and then replace them with a thought that does make you happy.

In a short time, you'll feel a "shift" inside of you that'll begin reminding you, *Only happy thoughts come from God, and I come from God, and those are the thoughts I will think about too.*

Dear God,

thank you for being so good to me and blessing me. I let go of the endless chatter and conversations I have with myself and of thinking about anything and anyone whom I have let upset me about anything. I give you my thoughts and thank you for making them about the things that make me happy and will prosper and bless me and everyone I meet. Thank you. Yes... Amen.

♥

> # *Why is it that one of the hardest things to do is be easy on yourself?"*

What does being a best friend mean to you?

Is it always being there when someone needs you?

Being kind, compassionate and loving?

Reminding someone of their greatness and the unlimited possibilities of who they can be?

Is it always letting go of the past and forgiving them of anything they've ever said or done?

That sounds like a pretty amazing best friend.

So why aren't you that same friend to yourself?

Bob will tell you I'm the best friend he's ever known, and I treat him and myself like that best friend all of the time.

There's never a day when I sit in the house or walk around the yard in a stupor, just brooding over past things I did.

I don't tell old unhappy stories to other dog buddies just so I can get a tail wiggle of support.

And I'll never replay anything in the past *unless* it makes me happy.

I love myself and my life and everything in it, and I give that love to everyone and everything I meet.

Just like you, I have a direct connection to God, and I always listen.

I live my life the way the divine voice of intuition inside of me speaks to me.

I'm easy on myself because that's the way I am created to be.

Just like you.

I've got some good news for you.

You don't need to be so demanding and difficult on yourself.

God will never ask you to be unhappy in order to receive a life filled and overflowing with goodness and blessings.

God's blessings are free.

And so is being kinder, more understanding and forgiving, and easy on yourself.

No one will treat you better than you treat yourself.

Be the best friend to yourself that you've ever known, and watch how the world starts treating you the same.

Dear God,

thank you for being so good to me. I'm so grateful that you love me with your divine perfect love even when I don't give myself that same love. It amazes me that after all these years, I'll sometimes have these feelings of unworthiness, guilt, and regret and that I should not or cannot receive your love, or another's love, or even my own love, because I don't deserve it. It's time to let all of that go. It's time for me to bless my past and all those in it and let it all go. Release it and them and let it all go to you so that I can open my heart and soul to let out the perfect divine child inside of me that is me. Let it all go so that I can fill my heart and overflow it with all the blessings to come into my life that you want to come into my life. Yes, dear God, the happy life I so want to live, love, and enjoy and share with others. Show me how to be my own best friend and to love that best friend with everything inside of me. Thank you. Yes... Amen.

♥

> # *How would you feel, if you didn't think so much about how you felt?"*

You humans spend so much time thinking about things that take away your happiness.

Like…

The past.

What someone said or did or didn't say or do.

Reacting to today's events and attaching labels and emotions to them and letting those emotions control your thoughts.

So here's question…

"How would you feel, if you didn't think so much about how you felt?"

I'll bet you'd feel *different*.

I'll bet you'd feel *happier*.

I'll bet you'd feel like a weight has been lifted from you.

The good news is you can feel all those things today if you'll let yourself.

Let me show you how.

You know what I think about?

The way I want to feel and always doing the things that make me happy.

I spend no time reminiscing about the past unless it makes me happy.

I spend zero time brooding over what someone said or did.

I never make up imagined things about my body or life that scare or worry me, or create and think about things that make me anxious or nervous.

I keep my thinking and attention *only* on the things I want and off of the things I don't want.

And I'm always the happiest boy dog you'll meet.

So why have *you* been making life so unnecessarily tough and difficult for *you*?

Why have you been so critical and demanding on yourself?

Why have you kept the things you desire and enjoy away from yourself?

God created you for great things, and enjoying your life is at the top of the list in your Owner's Manual of things you came here to do.

Give yourself a break.

Start being *good* to yourself again.

You deserve a life filled with wonderful things and experiences.

Every single day, you can have them!

It's time to let go of the endless thinking and critiquing about your life and start living and enjoying it.

And here's a little secret…

The less you think about how you feel, the more enjoyable your life will become.

Dear God,

for too long, I've been so demanding and tough on myself, and for what good reason? None! I'm shaking off the shackles of trying to please others. I'm letting go of trying to get others' approval. I'm saying goodbye to the endless critic inside of me who is never pleased and happy with anything I say or do and is always looking for things for me to feel bad about. None of that comes from you, God. It's all stuff that I've made up, and now I'm getting rid of it once and for all. The days and nights of feeling in a rut are over. I'm tired of looking down, and I'm now going to look up and out ahead in front of me at all the incredible things I can experience and enjoy. Thank you for showing me how to live my life filled with positive power, happy thoughts, joyful experiences, unlimited possibilities, and a head, heart, and soul overflowing with love. Thank you. Yes... Amen.

♥

You keep living with many beliefs that no longer benefit you"

What would it feel like to wake up each day and have no beliefs about anything except one—to have fun?

That's the way all of us dogs live.

Each day is a blank slate on our loving-this-life chalkboard, and the only goal and purpose is to have as much fun as we can.

The other animals we share our earth with are like that too.

They live for the moment and couldn't care less about anything else.

Everything in a dog's world is about love.

Loving you.

Loving life.

Loving this moment and having fun!

So why is that so hard for those in your people world to do the same?

I'll tell you.

You have so many beliefs about so many things that *keep* you from enjoying your life.

You imagine this or you worry about that, so it's no wonder you no longer laugh and have fun the way you used to.

Be kinder and nicer to yourself.

And give yourself a break!

God never feels hurt, anger, or disappointment about you, about anything, for any reason.

God is only love and forgives and forgets *any* and *everything* about your past and always will.

All of it.

No exceptions.

It's time to have more fun in your life.

It's time to be good to you again.

It's time to let go of the beliefs that no longer benefit you.

It's time to live and love your life.

Dear God,

I so greatly appreciate your showing me the things I believe and how those things either bring me joy and happiness or take them away. Right now, I give you any beliefs that no longer serve me, and I let all of those go so I can start thinking about the things that will prosper and bless me from this moment on. Thank you. Yes... Amen.

♥

> ## *How much of your time each day is going towards something you want or pushing against something you don't?"*

If someone asked how much time you spent yesterday thinking about things that made you uneasy, unhappy, or frustrated, what would you answer?

And if they asked me the same question, I'd answer, *"I spend no time thinking about any of it."*

And the reason is because *I never look back.*

As a dog, I am so fully focused and thinking about right now and the *next* right now.

What if you did the same?

What if you decided that today is the day you will not revisit the past or give any more thought to it?

Today you're just going to think about what you're doing *right now* and what you would like to do in your *next* right now.

Imagine how your life could dramatically change.

God is with you right here and now.

And God *isn't* tagging along with you whenever you decide to revisit the events and things that happened in the past.

It's over.

Shake the dust off your paws and walk on.

There is no need for you to worry about the next hour, the next day, or the next month.

God's got it and you all taken care of.

Dear God,

thank you for showing me how the past and those in it have been such amazing teachers. Everything that I have ever experienced always contains a blessing within it that has helped me to become who I am and has helped take me to where I am now. I know that life is a mirror and what I give out returns to me. I bless and send love to anyone and everyone in my life and let go of the past and only want the very best for anyone and everything that's ever been in it. I am so happy to begin this day fresh and brand new and for all the incredible opportunities and possibilities that are about to happen for me. Thank you. Yes... Amen.

♥

> # *You can have what you want... just stop telling yourself and others what you have that's not what you want"*

So many of you settle for a less-than-fulfilling life experience.

You accept what is given to you, what is handed down to you, and what you've always gotten, as the things you believe you'll always get.

In dog speak, you barely bark; and if you do, it's just a little whimper.

I love to bark, but just not at any and everything.

My bark has to mean something, and it always means something I believe.

My bark is like my words…

"Yes I want more of that!"

I let Bob and everyone know just what I believe, and I'm proud of it.

Words.

There is so much power in your words.

So few of you realize just what power the things you speak can and do bring into your life.

So few of you understand one of the most powerful divine principles you'll ever know…

You can have what you want… just stop telling yourself and others what you have that's not what you want.

The things you tell yourself have so much power.

The things you tell others have a God-releasing power that begins to move things for your benefit and good.

Things spoken on the outside confirm your beliefs on the inside.

And many times you have to speak it *out loud* before you begin to see it, feel it, and experience it in your life.

Yet what do so many of you do when you speak to others?

You tell them your problems, the things that make you unhappy, and the things you want to get rid of.

And then you encourage them to share with you the things that are upsetting them.

Talk about a feel-good experience.

Not!

That would be like Bob saying things to me that would make me unhappy.

Talking about things that would go so against how God created me that I would leave the room.

Not just leave the room, but wanting to be far, far away from such talk to get back to my balance, my God-center of happiness and joy, where I always live my life.

That never happens between us, and it never will.

It's time to stop letting it happen to you.

God is shining a light on you.

Quickly glance at your life and the lives of those others who are in your world right now.

You'll notice something awakening.

Rarely do you talk about the things you want and the things you believe you can have.

You spend more time thinking about and talking about the things you want to get rid of and those that bring you unhappiness.

There's an easier, simpler, better and happier way to live your life.

Believe more and bark louder and more often.

Talk about the things you want and, whether it's to yourself or others, talk about it only if makes you feel good.

Dear God,

thank you for showing me the life-changing power in the things I think and the words I speak. Help me to speak of possibilities and not problems. Help me to speak positive words of faith and hope and encouragement to those who need it. Thank you for bringing those into my life who will inspire, uplift, and empower my life and for allowing me to do the same for them. Let my words be filled with unlimited divine inspirations that will lift me, and all those who hear them, to a life greater than we have ever known. Thank you. Yes... Amen.

♥

Talk more about how you want it and less about how it was"

Have you ever met anyone who is always bringing up things that have gone wrong in their lives?

Things that happened years ago and are retold today like they just happened.

Your people world is full of good folks like this.

They've got so much time and emotional energy invested in telling how it *was*, that they have little desire to begin telling how'd they'd *like it to be*.

Dogs never tell a story.

I *live* a new story with the dawn on each new day.

And I let that day's story go at just the perfect time…

Just before Bob and I are about to go to sleep.

I'm thankful, grateful, and so appreciative of any and everything each day and at night just before bed, I give everything in it back to God.

Imagine that.

Whatever happened to you today, whatever you or anyone said or did or didn't do, is blessed and then released to God as your head hits your pillow.

As a dog, I don't care about the past because I always bark, tail-wiggle, and get excited about the things I want *now* and what's *to come*.

And you will be very wise if you do more of that too.

You have been given the power of speaking, and your words have incredible power.

When your words are used to build you up and get you excited, inspired, believing, and dreaming, those words release their God-moving power to change your life.

When you keep repeating what *was*, you are releasing your word power.

You're just releasing it to recreate your past in your *here and now* and in the *tomorrow* of your life.

If you want to start living a new kind of today and tomorrow, then do something easy...

Talk more about how you want it and less about how it was.

Dear God,

I bless everything and everyone in my past and let it and them go with blessings and love. Everything I've ever lived and anyone I've ever met have helped me to become who I am, and I'm so grateful for it all. I want to begin telling a new story, a happier story, an inspiring story of the person I desire to be and the life I desire to live. I know and believe my life can be as great as I allow it to be. I take the limits off of you and let go of any limitations, attitudes, and beliefs that have kept me where I am. Thank you for helping me to live the bigger, better, and most joyful life. You and I are the most powerful team, and together we can do amazing things that will touch people's lives for the best. Thank you. Yes... Amen.

♥

> # *It's time to get over how you were raised, so that you can be raised higher"*

Ask ten people you grew up with where they're now living, and most will tell you they live within 100 miles of where they grew up.

Ask those same ten people *why* they still live there, and many will tell you that it's home.

Translation: *It's what they know.*

The knowable, familiar, and predictable are the tethers that keep so many of those in your people world where they are and will keep them where they'll most likely always be.

There's nothing wrong with that *if* your life is filling up your life's purpose and passion tank.

It's when all you've ever known is accepted as all you *can* or *ever* will know, that's when this boy named Cody has a big lesson to share with you.

I came from a small crate.

It was the place where my beautiful mother raised me when I was just a newborn puppy.

I grew fast, and so did my awareness, awakening, acceptance, and understanding placed within me by God, that a bigger, better, and more amazing life awaited me…

Just outside the crate.

Never once have I looked back, thought back, or wanted to go back to the crate I grew up in during the first weeks of my life as a puppy, just because *that's* where I came from and *that's* all I ever knew.

I never latched on to the all-too-often repeated excuses people believe of *why* I couldn't move or *have* a different life.

I embrace and love the unknown.

I live my life by faith and trust, knowing that the God who created me will always be there with me and in me, guiding, protecting, and blessing me.

God wants to do the same for you.

Regardless of your past, regardless of your age, regardless of the decisions and mistakes you think you've made that you keep beating yourself up over, year after year after year.

Let all of that go, because none of it matters.

Your *past* has nothing to do with your *future*.

To go from where you are to where God *can* and *wants* to take you, simply begin by doing one thing…

Keep the things from your childhood that have and still continue to help you, and let go of everything else.

God wants to *raise* you.

Raise you up to a *better* life.

Raise you up to a *bigger* life.

Raise you up to a more *prosperous* life.

Raise you up to a more *satisfying* life.

Raise you up to a more *fulfilling* life.

Raise you up to a *happier* and more *joyful* life.

Raise you up to a life of *purpose*, *power*, and *passion* so that you can be living your life in a fresh, brand new way.

By and from the inspiration of God.

Dear God,

help me to know what living a bigger, better, and no-limits life can feel like. I let go of the limits I've placed upon myself. I ask that you fill my life with new blessings, abundance, greatness, and inspiration, plus the desire to do more, be more, experience more, enjoy more, and love more. Help me to believe bigger and live greater than I've ever known. With you, all things are possible. Thank you. Yes... Amen.

♥

Compare? Don't you dare!"

If anyone ever asked a dog, "What's the best way for me to feel unhappy about myself and my life?" we'd give the same one-word answer…

"Compare."

Compare your life, looks, money, possessions, and accomplishments to others, and unhappiness will always be the result.

As a dog, I never compare anything about my life and me to any other dog or person.

All I care about is my world and loving all those and everything in it.

That's how God is too.

All of us are loved the same, with no exceptions.

Having a bigger home, nicer cars, or walls of merit badges, accolades, and awards doesn't do anything to change how much you are already loved and will always be loved.

God's love was 100 percent unconditional love the moment you were created, and it is and will always be unconditional, all the days and nights of your life.

Let this sink in…

You are a one-of-a-kind priceless masterpiece whose unconditional love and acceptance is guaranteed and whose greatness is ready for you to be realized.

No other person anywhere in the world will look or be like you.

Not one.

Ever.

It's time for you to shine.

It's time for you to smile.

It's time to start living the life you dream, and the time to begin it is now.

Dear God,

thank you for this great day and all the blessings you have given to me. Thank you for taking away the belief that the tougher I am on myself, the more you and others will love me. I know that is never true and will never be true. Your love is unconditional, and I want my love of me and for others to be the same too. You are amazing. I am amazing. We are all amazing. Thank you. Yes… Amen.

♥

> ## *Other people's opinions will never be more important than your own"*

Why is that those in your people world value more what other people say and think about them than what they think about themselves?

When it comes to caring what anyone else thinks of me, Bob knows I have it figured out.

You see, I love anyone and everyone, but no one or no thing is more important than *me* being happy.

You can ask Bob; he'll tell you that everything I think or do is *always* in the direction of those things that bring me happiness and joy.

Early in your lives, so many of you were taught by other people that to seek your own happiness was selfish and it was more important that you put the needs and happiness of other people first before your own.

And you did, because receiving other's approval was what you believed you needed so *you* could feel happier.

We dogs have something to tell you…

God will not have any of that.

God created you as a divine perfect child in every way.

You are complete, perfect, and unconditionally loved just the way you look and are *this moment*.

Be true to how you've been created and to who and what you are, and I can assure you that your happiness will be guaranteed.

Dear God,

I am thankful you are so loving, kind, and understanding with me. Oh, how I have spent too much time caring what others think about me and how it feels so empty and less than who I am each time I do. Thank you for showing that to me. Help me to trust myself more and more with each new day. Show me how to trust and rely on your perfect guidance and to listen to the voice inside of me that is your guidance and inspiration. Thank you. Yes... Amen.

♥

Worry yourself about none of it, because God is taking care of all of it"

Who taught you humans to worry, and why do you spend so much time doing it?

Bob and I have been together for years and not once have I worried about *anything*.

As a dog, I know nothing about what it means to worry.

You humans do, and just look at how doing so affects your happiness.

I love life and live it with such enthusiasm, joy, and excitement that every moment is the next great adventure I can't wait to live and experience.

What if you lived more of your life like that?

You can.

And I'm about to show you how.

First, let me ask you something.

Do you ever wonder if God worries?

After all, God made everything and controls it all, so what would God have to worry about?

I'll tell you…

Nothing.

Absolutely nothing.

So why not you?

After all, God made *you* and knows everything you'll ever need, even *before* you know it, and knows the best way to get you from where you are to where you want to be.

So what's there to ever worry about?

Not a single thing.

For the next hour, try doing what I do.

Try living your life without any worries. Then try another hour and another.

Soon, you'll be going through most of your day (if not all of it) worrying about *nothing*.

And what a relief that's going to be for you!

The things you worry about are imagined, and so is the great life that can be yours.

Imagine it big, imagine it beautiful, and imagine it wonderful.

It's about to be!

Dear God,

thank you for showing me that you know nothing about worry and that I can be like you and not worry too. Help me to let go of anything that takes away my happiness and joy. Thank you for filling my life with only the things you want to bless me with, for they will only be those that will make me happy and are in divine perfect harmony with your plan and purpose for my life. Thank you. Yes... Amen.

♥

> ## *There's a big difference between what you'd like to experience and what you believe you can experience*"

In your lifetime, you'll meet many people.

Some will live lives that'll inspire you, and others not so much.

All of you will have things you'd *like* to do.

In fact, you can make lists full of them.

Then there are the things you *believe* you can do.

That's a *much* smaller list.

There is a *big* difference between what you'd *like* to have and what you *believe* you can have.

It's the things you *believe* you can be, do, or have that guide your actions, experiences, results, and life.

Bob will tell you that I've never made a list.

I don't need to.

I like what I believe and believe what I like.

And I always experience a life of joy and happiness because there's never any difference between the two.

Every day a new desire is born inside of me.

Every day I give birth to that desire by believing in it and letting myself go to it and live it.

How about you?

Have you let your old beliefs determine how big your *new* dreams and desires will be?

Be honest.

God knows the answer.

And so do you.

Start turning those "What I'd like to have" into "What I *believe* I can have" by letting yourself live a bigger and better life.

God created you to live a life without limits.

You are the only one who puts those big, new and wonderful things and experiences in your life by what you *believe* and what you feel *worthy* to receive.

It's time to take the limits off of God and step out of the old limited life you've been living and into the new and extraordinary life that's waiting for you.

Dear God,

thank you for showing me how to dream a bigger dream. Thank you for calling and inspiring me to become higher, be better, be more, and live a life filled with love for you, me, this life, and everyone I meet. Help me to change my thinking from what I'd 'like' to be, do, and have to what I 'believe' I can be, do, and have. With you, dear God, all things are possible. With you, I can do all things because your strength, power, wisdom, wellbeing, love, and blessings are always inside of me and surround me wherever I am and wherever I go. We are best friends and soulmates. I love you. Thank you. Yes... Amen.

♥

Just because you can't hear it or smell it doesn't mean it's not real"

Ever see love before?

No one has.

Yet you *know* it's real.

For a lot of those in your people world, that's not enough.

Many of you live by the belief that you need to be *shown* things that others say are true before you'll *believe* it so for yourself.

We dogs didn't get the memo on that one.

I have amazing eyes that can see anything and everything near and far.

But that's only a fraction of my God-given abilities.

I have even more amazing eyes that know and can see on *the inside* the things that can't be seen on the outside.

Things like…

Trust.

Belief.

Assurance.

Knowing.

Guidance.

Wellbeing.

Love.

The things that come from God.

So how can you be like more like us dogs and experience those things for yourself?

It's easier than you may think.

Start by doing two things.

Trust and believe.

The greatest power you'll ever know and experience is that which comes from *the unseen.*

Every dream you have is born in *the unseen.*

Every idea you have begins inside of you from *the unseen.*

Every ounce of love you feel and will ever feel comes from an inexhaustible *unseen* reservoir that knows no limits.

Just try reaching the end of your ability to love, and you'll never find it.

I *live* it.

I *love* it.

So does Bob.

And so can you.

The seed that became you began in the spirit, which became the you that you see and the you that others know.

Greatness always begins in the unseen.

Let yourself be bigger and greater than you are.

God's *unseen* is ready to become your *lived and known.*

Dear God,

your power is simply amazing, and what's even more astounding is that I come from you. You created me! Thank you! Help me to increase my faith and belief in your unseen and unknown so that I may live a life of greatness, happiness, love, inspiration, and joy that I, and others, may know and be positively touched by. I feel your presence inside and all around me, God. I am yours. Thank you. Yes... Amen.

♥

I know nothing of..."

Words.

How is it that something you can't see, smell, taste, or touch can have so much power over what you feel and experience?

The things people are told and taught as young kids can stay with them all of their lives.

For many of those in your people world, it can take sixty years to get over their first six.

How different would your life be if you never heard a negative or limiting word?

How different would your life feel if you were never taught a limiting belief, idea, or action?

How different would you think if the pure innocent child you came into this world being, remained untouched as the pure innocent child you *still* are?

Bob will tell you I'm his living proof of all of that every single day.

Like all dogs, my unconditional love, purity, innocence, excitement, sense of wonder, acceptance, and everything about me shows Bob that, whenever he looks at me, he's *looking at the purest four-legged creation of God on this earth.*

That's who *we* dogs are.

That's who *you* are.

I and all the dogs you love are God's messengers to you.

And we have something to teach you.

We carry the message to you that says...

I know nothing of guilt.

I know nothing of regret.

I know nothing of remorse.

I know nothing of sin.

I know nothing of lack.

I know nothing of limitation.

I know nothing of unhappiness.

I know nothing of anger.

I know nothing of resentment.

I know nothing of forgiveness because there's nothing to forgive.

All I know is love, and that's how God created you.

Dear God,

you created me to be pure love, and that's what I am and will always be. As a child of yours, I'm made in your image. You created me for so many reasons, and nothing in this life is by randomness or chance. You are directing it all. I give you my life and everything in it so you can guide it to every blessing and every divinely inspired desire you give me that will always be for my divine perfect, highest, best good. Yes, I thank you for all my amazing blessings. I thank you for the gift of my life and for every moment of every day. I let go of any feelings and beliefs of unworthiness and in their place I fill my life with love for me and for anyone and everyone else I meet. Thank you. Yes… Amen.

♥

I live in a world of 'Yes' and "Thank you'"

Imagine living your life by three important words: *"Yes"* and *"Thank you."*

"Yes" because you only keep your thinking and beliefs on the things you *want*, and *"Thank you"* because God keeps pouring into your life *only* the things that you *want*.

I know exactly what this kind of life feels like because I live it all of the time.

I don't know what it feels like to have guilt, regret, remorse, lack, limitation, fear, doubt, worry, anxiety, uncertainty, or any other feeling those in your people world experience that isn't a happy feeling.

I only know *"I like this"* and *"I'll take more of this... Thank you."*

That's my belief, and God always answers my belief by giving me only the things that match it.

You *can live in that same kind of world.*

You just have to let go of the unhappy world you've been spending your life in for way too long.

Begin today and start saying more *"Yeses"* and *"Thank you's,"* and your world and the life you live will begin to shift in ways that are going to make you *very* happy.

Dear God,

I say "Yes" and Thank you" for every blessing in my life and all the new blessings and happy joyful experiences that are on the way to me. Help me to keep my thoughts and words on the things I want. I let go of the people and things that I've let hurt, anger, or upset me, or bring me unhappiness in any way, and wish them only love and blessings as I release them all. I fill my life with your divine perfect gifts and thoughts and, as I do, I feel my life getting better and better, every day and in every way. Thank you. Yes... Amen.

♥

There is always a door that's open for you"

How quickly those in your people world stop, when they are met with opposition at the doors of their desires.

Most will stop trying after the first, second, or third attempt.

Fewer others will continue to go on until they reach the fourth, fifth, or sixth go at it.

Fewer still will keep believing and trying beyond the seventh, eighth, ninth, or tenth try.

The fewest of you will keep on keeping on until they reach their desired result.

I am one of them.

I never stop at the first shut door.

Or any door.

I stay excited and don't care what's in my way.

I keep going to the next door and the next until I find *the* door, the *perfect* door, that's open, ready, and waiting for me to walk through it.

And I always find what I'm looking for and even better things I never expect.

All because I never stop believing there's a door that will always be open and waiting for me.

That's just the way God created you.

Who cares if you don't know, can't know, or won't know all the doors you'll try and go through on the road to whatever you desire?

Who cares if you don't know, can't know, or won't know all the people you'll meet and the things that are going to happen on the way to your dream?

Go as far as you can, and once you get there you'll be able to see further.

The things you can experience, be, do, or have are endless.

One door leads to the next door.

One contact leads to the next contact.

One joy leads to the next joy.

It is God's Never Ending that will always be Never Ending.

Don't stop at the first door.

There's another one that's open and waiting for you just up ahead.

Dear God,

thank you for the dreams and desires you give me. I know that you are my creator, protector, provider, and best friend and that you always have, and will always have, my divine best interests at the top of everything you do in my life. Starting today, I will have a new belief, faith, and trust in you to take me to every dream I have and to those I've yet to dream of, all in your divine perfect way and timing. You are amazing. I love you. Thank you. Yes... Amen.

♥

Because I always believed it"

As you go through life, there'll be times when wonderful, unexpected things happen to you and you'll be so happily surprised.

There will be times when the things you want will fall quickly and easily into place and you'll be thrilled.

And there will be times, when you've got a belief so big and so grand that you've had for so long, when years may go by before you'll ever see *any* hint that it will happen.

Oh.

But when it does…

Get ready because the tidal wave of blessings, abundance, and opportunities will happen so quickly and be so great, that it's going to surprise you.

And stun others.

They may ask, *"How did all of this happen?"* and you'll reply, *"Because I always believed it."*

Bob will tell you that I'm his daily living, breathing, and walking reminder of just what it's like to live your life by belief.

Belief in the unknown.

Belief in the unseen.

Belief in the uncertain.

Belief in the God that created me.

I never doubt what I believe because I never have any reason to.

Whatever I desire, God takes me to it, and I always go where I'm divinely led because I believe.

And God always rewards those who believe.

It's easy to believe in the things that make you unhappy.

That's what most people that we dogs meet will do.

So why is it so hard to believe in the things that can bring you joy and change your life for the better?

So many of those in your people world want to see proof before they'll make a commitment or decision to anything or anyone.

Yet what if, for years, the only proof you'd ever see that life was on the way to changing to become amazing for you, was *just the belief you had* that it would?

It's easy to believe in the things that are given to you.

It takes faith to believe in the things that are on the way to you.

Start living your life with more of that faith and belief.

Believe good things are on the way to you, and they soon will be.

Believe the right people will be put into your life at just the right time and for just the right reason, and they soon will be.

Believe God wants to give you a bigger, richer, more beautiful and enjoyable life, and soon you will start living it.

Expect the best to happen to you, and it will.

And when all those people see how quickly and dramatically everything in your life is just falling so beautifully into place and they ask, *"How did all of this happen?"*

You'll just smile and say, *"Because I always believed it."*

Dear God,

I am so grateful and thankful for the ability you have given to me to have faith, to trust, and to believe. For so long, I've believed in the life I've been living and that belief has kept creating the life I've been living. I'm ready to change that. I'm ready to trust again. Trust you, trust me, and trust us to make my life the amazing and blessed masterpiece you've created it and me to be. Take me to all the great and good you know I dream of and desire, and to the phenomenal I don't even know about yet and you do. Together, we are unstoppable. We are the best team. Let's touch the world with the gifts, talents, and abilities you've blessed me with. Let's make people's lives better in all the ways we can. I'm yours. I love you, dear God. Thank you. Yes… Amen.

♥

What you want is just a stretch away"

Those in your people world would be surprised.

Surprised to know just how *close* they came to the things they wanted before they gave up right before those things were ready to happen.

Just a *little* longer.

Just a *little* more effort.

Just a *little* more belief they were on the way and about to happen, would've been *all* that was needed to change their lives forever.

For many of you, you're always on the cusp and the edge of something really great about to happen.

Then you get in the way.

You cherish the comfort zone so much, that rarely do you enter and allow yourself to visit *the stretch zone,* where so many of the things and experiences you want are just waiting for you.

Simply for the price of an effort to stretch yourself from what is *to* what can be.

I love to stretch.

Not just my body, also my life.

And I make it a point to do so every day.

Many times, I'll be outside having such fun and then I'll see, smell, or hear something that makes me drop everything and follow that new desire to wherever it's now leading me.

Once I find it, many times it might be out of reach from where I'm presently standing.

Does that stop me?

Not even a chance.

When I know I want something and that something is just beyond my reach and grasp, never once do I stop and turn around and think, *"Too bad it's not right here in front of me so I can just bend down and pick it up. I guess I'll just let it go."*

Let it go, like so many of you do, and go back to what you've been doing for far too long in your life because you won't stretch and go after it.

I stretch and stretch, and I never stop stretching *until* I grab it.

And I always do.

So how about you?

When was the last time you *stretched*?

Stretched your *thinking*?

Stretched your *beliefs*?

Stretched your *faith*?

Stretched your actions and gone beyond what you've always done, to a new place where you pushed yourself a little more to a whole new level?

It only takes just a little to change your life a lot.

The things you dream of, desire, and want are calling you to them.

It's time for you to grab them and enjoy them.

And they're only a stretch away.

Dear God,

thank you for taking me out of the comfort zone and into the kind of thinking, ideas, faith, belief, and expectation that bring me to the greater life that's waiting for me outside that comfort zone. The place where your blessings and experiences are waiting for me to live, love, and enjoy. Help me to grow, be, do, and become all that you've created me to be. I take the limits off of you, dear God, and I'm ready for us to create the best life you have planned for me that can only come from you. Together we are unstoppable. Thank you. Yes... Amen.

♥

Never let your tail stop wiggling"

You know, when you're a dog, it's just impossible for you to hide how you feel.

Take being happy.

Good luck trying to find a dog that's happy and *not* wagging and wiggling its tail.

It's impossible!

Just ask me.

My tail is my always-on truth detector, and that tail is always wiggling from first thing in the morning to the last thing at night before Bob and I go to bed.

All because I'm happy.

I'm *always* the happy puppy, regardless of my age.

Seeing that happy boy puppy in me that I always am is a constant reminder to Bob of a very powerful lesson I love showing him.

This is the way life can always be when you're not thinking of the things in your life that you've let upset you.

It's time to let go of those old hurts, anger, frustration, doubts, worries, regrets, remorse, and anything and anyone that takes away from your joy and happiness.

God created you to be happy.

Give yourself that gift and your tail will *always* be wiggling.

Dear God,

I know that you've given me my life so that I can love and enjoy it. Thank you for it. I'm so grateful for all the things that make me happy and for all the things that are about to make me happy. I let go of thinking about anyone and anything that takes away my joy. In its place, I fill my life with happy thoughts, loving thoughts, empowering thoughts, and thoughts that fill me with your peace and presence. Thank you. Yes... Amen.

♥

2

A BEST
FRIEND CALLED
YOUR PAST

Then was so needed to get you to now"

Can I tell you something that's going to make you feel better?

Every person you will meet has made a mistake.

People all make mistakes—lots of mistakes.

So smile.

It's just a part of your being a human.

Mistakes teach you so much.

They can be amazing friends as they show you how you can do better next time.

If you asked any dog if we've ever made a mistake, we'd tell you, *"Not a single one."*

And it would be true.

You see, everything we do is on purpose. And because it's on purpose, it's always the right thing for us to do at that moment in our life.

I know the things that bring me the greatest joy and happiness, and I do those.

I let everything else go.

I live by the attitude that *"The more I grow, the more I let the unimportant stuff go."*

I'm not looking to do anything over again because I don't need to.

I instantly let whatever happens go, and then I forget about it.

I'm only interested in *right now*, and I can't wait to get to that next *right now*.

How about you?

Do you hold onto things too long, or can you quickly and easily let them go?

Letting go is the happy way to live your life because…

Trying to fix past mistakes or regrets rarely results in a happy "right now" experience.

Think about your life and how much happier you'd be if you stopped caring so much about what you said or did back *then*.

Then was so needed to get you to now.

Bless your past.

Release it.

Then think about it no more.

You've got an amazing life just waiting for you to live and love.

Dear God,

I am so thankful for everything that has happened to me because it's all helped me to become who I am and get me to where I stand right now. I bless all of the people and experiences that have been my teachers on this journey of life so far. I know that an amazing life of the right people and experiences are just waiting for me to discover. I'm so grateful that you're taking me to them and them to me in your divine perfect way. Thank you. Yes… Amen.

♥

Regret nothing. Bless everything."

If only you could just have a do over.

One more chance to go back and say it, do it, and get it right.

So many of those in your people world carry the guilt and remorse of regret for things and people they think they've done wrong in the past.

They carry it inside of them for years.

They carry it for so long as it slowly takes away any joy and happiness that may come their way.

The believed past wrongs cause them to feel unworthy to receive the blessings and good God sends to them.

It's time for that baggage and those attitudes to stop.

It's time for you to *regret nothing and bless everything.*

In the world of Cody, that's me, you'll never find anything to be regretful, remorseful, angry, worrisome, or doubtful over.

There are no regrets, because everything that has, is, or ever will be done or said is for a purpose.

A divine purpose.

Even when you cannot fathom what it is, that purpose *always* carries a blessing for you and everyone who experiences any part of it.

Wherever you are in your life and whatever you may have experienced, you can be sure of this...

Everything and everyone in your life helped you to become who you are right now.

And you helped do the same thing for them.

Take any one of those past experiences or people away from your past, and you would not be who you are and where you are.

Look back at anything that's ever happened to you.

At the time you experienced and went through it, you had no idea how anything called "good" could ever come as a result of it.

Ah…

But look at you now.

Years ahead and so much farther on the road of your life's journey you now are, and not only can you see *the* blessing, you can see *many* of them!

All because of what you experienced *then*.

God created us because we are teachers and helpers to and for each other.

We are built for each other.

As God's teachers, we are here to help each other experience, learn, and grow into the blessed angels we are and those that God is forever creating us to be.

You have nothing to be regretful over.

Nothing.

It's time for you to let the past go.

Let every bit of it go.

Bless it. Love it. Now leave it.

Dear God,

I'm so thankful for everything and everyone who has been in my past. I bless them, love them, and thank them and you for bringing all things and people who always work together for your and our divine perfect, highest, best good. Thank you for showing me how to move on and let go of my past so that I may live my life to the fullest and happiest today and all the days to come. I choose to spend my time thinking on the things and experiences I want and being so happy about today and tomorrow, for I know that's where I will be living the rest of my life. I'm so excited for all the things and blessings and experiences you have planned for me and for us to experience together. My life is incredible, and it's only going to get better. And it's all because of you. Thank you. Yes... Amen.

♥

Everything is perfectly choreographed in your life"

Can I tell you a little secret?

There are no accidents in this life of yours.

Everything in your life happens for a reason.

The right people come into your life at just the right time to give you (and you to give them) a piece you both need that helps each of you move forward to the next place you want to go on your life's journey.

Some people are in your life for a long time.

Others may be only there for a few seconds, but those few seconds will give you a thought, a word, a smile, or an inspiration that will help you in ways you may not realize at the moment but later will, as you look back on how things unfolded and happened.

As a dog, I love knowing and living my life like this.

Each day, I anticipate God's perfect timing and orchestrating of things in my life, and I'm *never* disappointed.

Let me tell you a story to show you just what I mean…

One day, Bob and I went bye-bye in our car for a bite to eat, and we decided to try a different restaurant we hadn't been to in a while.

At the very same time we were there, so were the owners of a Weimaraner dog I would have so much fun playing with.

Think about it.

If Bob and I had chosen a different restaurant, left at a different day or time, been delayed in getting there by only a few minutes, meeting my new four-legged buddy would've never happened.

Yet it did.

And it's all because of God.

That's the way it can be for your life too.

It's not too late.

You are not too old, nor have you made too many mistakes.

There are no delays.

Everything about your life is right on plan.

God's plan.

Here's something you're going to love.

Today and tomorrow, notice how many things happen that *seem* like a coincidence.

Pay attention to the people you see and meet.

Listen to what they say, whether it's to you or to others.

Start looking for the connection between those people and the things that happen to the things you've been thinking about—*especially your goals and dreams.*

Like me, and what I always show Bob, you're going to find that God is with you *everywhere* you go and helping you in ways that will simply astonish and amaze you.

Dear God,

thank you for showing me the ways you are with me, guiding me, helping me and orchestrating everything in my life. I am so grateful for it all. I know and believe you created me for a special purpose—actually, many of them. I thank you for showing me all the reasons you created me and for helping me to become all that you know I can be. I let go of anything that keeps me from having and enjoying the best life and the blessings you have for me, and I trust your divine perfect plan for every part of my life. Thank you. Yes... Amen.

♥

Never be afraid to change anything in your life"

One of the most difficult things in life is change.

Those in your human world like the comfortable, the knowable, and the predictable.

And you'll sacrifice the possibility of the new and exciting, just so you can stay in the familiar.

As a dog, I don't care about any of that.

Every moment I can, I'm exploring and finding what is new, fresh, and undiscovered, and I never give any thoughts to what *might* be.

All I care about is what's *ahead,* and that's the direction where I want to point my head.

Just like God.

God never looks back.

God is always focused with us in the here and now and is already *there* wherever we want to go.

To go there requires just one thing: *Let go of the old so the new can come into your life.*

Start to trust yourself more.

Have more faith in yourself.

Listen to your inner calling and follow it whenever and wherever it leads you.

That calling inside of you will always be just what you need and at just the right time in your life that you need it.

Dear God,

I am so grateful for the desires you have placed inside of me. I know that the calling from you to a bigger, greater, and better life will never end, and I am so thankful for it. Thank you for helping me to let go of my fear of the unknown. Help me to replace my fears with faith and trust as you guide my life perfectly and divinely to anyone and everything for my divine perfect, highest, best good. Thank you. Yes... Amen.

♥

Keep the past in your present if it brings you happiness and joy"

Those in your people world say lots of things.

Especially when they talk about the past and present.

How many times have you read or heard someone say, "You've got to let go of the past" or "That was then and this is now"?

Yes, today is a brand new day where you can do anything you dream of and experience whatever you desire.

Today is also the day you can feel happiness and joy.

Not just for the new that awaits you, but for the past that has touched you.

A happy life is made up of the people and things that bring you joy and happiness and make you smile.

Many of those things are things you've already lived and loved.

Including animals and people.

I love exploring the new, whether it's a new stick, a new trail filled with new sights and sounds and smells, a new bird or squirrel to bark at and chase, and anything else.

I love when Bob and I go bye-bye in our car and all the new things we see, smell and hear as I stick my happy boy head out the window with the biggest smile on my face.

I also love those things in my past.

Yes, even we dogs have pasts that we love.

Like an old well-worn and traveled path and trail that always makes me happy every time I walk along it.

I love those familiar ponds, rivers, and the ocean I love to swim in and the dogs I love to see and play with.

Those things in my *yesterday* that always bring me such joy *today*.

Never be afraid or regretful of your past.

Look at your past and, if any of it made you happy and still does, then don't let go of what helped you to grow.

Cherish it.

Bless it.

And keep on loving it.

Dear God,

thank you for showing me how to make peace with my past and bless all those who have been a part of it. Each experience and each person gave me the perfect piece I needed at that time in my life to help me grow and move my thinking, believing, and life to the next step it needed to go and be. Help me keep my thoughts filled and overflowing with only the good, the positive, the inspiring, the encouraging, the hopeful, and the joyful. Thank you for showing me that a happy life is made up of happy thoughts and moments. Every day and in every way, my life keeps getting better and better. I'm so grateful for all of your help and blessings. I love you dear God. Thank you. Yes... Amen.

♥

> ## *Make the last experience of what you do a happy one, and you'll remember it for the rest of your life"*

Go back to a happy time when you did something you really loved.

Years may go by; yet, whenever you think about the experience again, it *always* makes you happy.

Ever wonder why that is?

I knew the answer early on when I was just a pup.

I always look for new things to explore, to try, and to do that will make me happy, and I find them every moment of my life.

Like me, you were created by God to be here and live your life not for the hardship and struggle of it, but for the *joy, exhilaration,* and *thrill* of it.

Many of those in your people world simply can't imagine what a happy and joyful life would be like.

They've become so used to staying in their comfort zone and living a life of boredom and routine monotony that they won't let themselves "go there" and think about what their life *could* be like.

It doesn't have to be that way.

God is always calling you.

Calling you to where your next great happy experiences are waiting for you.

We dogs should know.

We go there and live it every day.

Today is the day you can experience it too.

Dear God,

thank you for helping me be nicer, kinder, and better to myself. Thank you for helping me stop being so tough on myself and to stop beating myself up for not being this imaginary perfect person I've believed I should be. I know you see me as divinely created and just perfect as I am and will always be. I am so grateful for your showing me how to focus on the things that make me happy and all the new things you want me to experience, enjoy, and be blessed with. You are so good to me. Thank you. Yes… Amen.

♥

> *Keep looking forward,*
> *because that's where all*
> *the good stuff is"*

For so many of you, living your lives in the past is so much easier than thinking about some imagined wonderful future.

Yet doing so is like walking forward with your head always turned around and looking behind you.

As dogs, we don't do that.

I always know where to find the good stuff.

The new sights and sounds and smells and experiences I want are always in one place.

Just up ahead.

And that's where I keep my head.

Always looking forward.

Just like God.

Whatever Bob and I do, wherever we go, I love showing Bob how I'm always looking forward and ahead, because that's where *the next* fun experience is to be found.

Like sticking my head as far as I can out of our car windows!

And just look at how many other dogs do it too!

The excitement is for the things in front of me that I want and not the things in the past and behind me that I've already let go.

God made all us dogs to instinctively know this.

And for good reason.

God doesn't care or think about the past for one nanosecond.

It's all about being in the *now*, the right *here*, and in this *moment*.

And God is already in your *next* moment.

At the place you like to call *the future.*

Already there and ready for you to come and experience the fun of it too.

Our creator never remembers, condemns, or holds anything against us, whether it was back then, right now, or at any time in the future.

God never regrets, feels sorry for, feels guilty about, or wishes for a do-over about *anything.*

So why do you?

There are not enough people you could go back to and call and apologize for anything you said or did.

There are not enough "sorry's", "sure wish I wouldn't have done that's", or "wish I would've done better's" you could go back and say, that will make you feel better for any mistakes, misjudgments, wrongs, regrets, guilt, or anything that causes you to feel badly.

The good news is…

You don't need to!

Let the past go with love, kindness, and forgiveness to you and to others.

It's time to stop looking at your *past* through the eyes and wisdom and understanding that you have *today.*

You are a very different person *today* than you were back *then.*

You did whatever you did because you thought it was the best you knew how to do at the time.

Every mistake you thought and believed you may have made has helped you to become better and who and what you are today.

In other words…

It was all *good!*

Each day I show Bob this powerful lesson: *Keep your mind on things you want and off of the things you don't.*

It is time for you to be more like us dogs.

It's time to turn your head around and start looking forward, and only forward, to what's out in front of you and waiting for you just up ahead.

You're soon about to discover that's where all the good stuff is.

Dear God,

I so appreciate your showing me how the past was my teacher and how today and tomorrow are the places where I'm going to live and love the rest of my life. I bless and love anyone, everyone, and every experience I've ever had. Today is brand new, and so will be my every tomorrow. I want to live and enjoy them from where I now am and where you're going to take me to where I soon will be. I love you and am so grateful to you. Thank you. Yes... Amen.

♥

> ## *When looking back on your life, just remember... that was then, but this is Wow!"*

I know.

You've gone through some tough times.

Times so tough, that you had no idea how and when they would end and what, if any, good could possibly come out of such difficulty.

But they did end.

And so many good lessons came out of it.

Lessons and experiences you needed to get you to a better place in your life along with the good and blessings you are enjoying today.

In your people world, time is such a wonderful and patient teacher.

When you look back on your life, you can now say and mean it, *"Yes, that was then, but this is Wow!"*

The good news is…

God has a lifetime of "Wows" still waiting for you.

I love living in the *now* because that's where I find the next great experience called "*Wow!*"

For me, the past is only and will always be the past.

It's like a wind that blows past me and then is forever off and gone, never to be repeated and experienced again.

I experience the moment of it, at that specific time in my life, and I don't spend any time chasing it or thinking about it again.

That's the way God does things.

God is all about *Here's the experience you need at this time in your life, and as soon as you get it and learn it, then that experience is going to leave you.*

So why do so many of those in your people world keep clinging to the people and experiences of the past, those that God wants you to let go of, so you can move on and to the next place God wants to take you?

Do you really think that if you spend enough time thinking about something, regretting it, feeling guilty, ashamed, remorseful, angry, or hurt over what happened back then, that you can somehow change the experience and outcome of it?

Please.

Not even a chance!

Nor would you want to, because there's never ever any happiness to be found in doing so.

Let what happened *then* be released, forgiven, and forgotten.

And let it be so *now*.

God has such an amazing life waiting for you.

And that amazing life doesn't care who you are, what you did or did not do, what your age, race, gender or anything else is.

You are God's priceless creation.

And God created you for a purpose.

Actually, lots of them that are going to surprise you.

So let go of the past.

Yes, let it go so you can grow.

That was then and this day and all the days to come are going to be your *Wow*.

Dear God,

I am so ready to live a new life of Wows. What happened back then will always be what happened back then and has nothing to do with me today, tomorrow, or any of the days that will be waiting for me to live, love, enjoy, and discover. I thank you for being so understanding and loving with me. You know, better than I or anyone else, that I always want and try and do the very best I can at the time I'm doing it. And you always whisper to me, with the voice within that I know comes from you, that the best I can do and know at the time I think about and do it, will always be just perfect, because you wouldn't allow anything to happen in my life unless it is for my divine perfect and highest, best good, and according to your plan for me and my life. You know, dear God, the more I think about it, the more I realize something amazing: I've never made any mistakes! Everything and everyone that's ever been or will ever be a part of my life in any way, is there and will be there for a divine reason and because it all fits perfectly into your divinely amazing plan for this gift you've given me called My Life! I love you so much, God. Thank you with all of my heart and soul for everyone and everything. I bless and love it and them all! Thank you. Yes... Amen.

♥

3

THE GIFT
OF PEOPLE IN
YOUR LIFE

Family and friends see you as the way you were and not as the way you are and have become"

In your people world, friends and family can be one of the greatest mirrors you'll ever have.

They reflect back to you who they are, what they believe, and how they've made up their minds to see you.

You could go years without seeing your family.

During those years and time away, your life could change dramatically.

During those years, the seismic changes within you for the best would be astonishing to those who didn't have a history with you or thought they knew you so well.

Ah…

Yet the moment you come back home and see family again, nothing will have changed.

At least to them.

They'll still be talking about the same old things they've been talking about every year.

And for many, they'll rarely, if ever ask, *"What's new and wonderful in your life?"*

We dogs see it all the time.

People who think they know you don't want to know what's changed with you because so little has changed for them.

They don't want to know about the new and good in your life, when their deeply entrenched attitudes and beliefs about you have never changed.

Their attitudes, beliefs, and how comfortable they feel treating you the way they do was set *years* ago.

And rarely, if ever, will they change.

Not because they can't.

Because they won't.

It makes Bob so happy I'll never be like those kinds of old friends and family.

I live with Bob night and day and I always see Bob as who he is at *that* moment, each moment we're together.

I never have preconceived notions about anything or anyone.

I live by the attitude of *"Every moment is a new moment, and that's how I'm going to love and treat you."*

And I always do.

Just like God.

Imagine if you were more dog-like and God-like in the ways you look at and treat those you *believe* you know so well.

Your world would change.

Their world would change.

Big time.

And all of it, for the happier and better.

Here's something fun to try.

Next time you're with those old friends and family, try something that's going to surprise them.

Treat them like someone you've just met.

They're not the same people they were last year.

And neither are you.

Dear God,

I am so grateful and appreciate everything and everyone in my life. I release the old attitudes and beliefs about anyone and anything. Each day is a brand new day and with it, I'm created new. Thank you for helping me to grow in positive, loving, inspiring, and empowering ways. I let go of the old so that the new you want to bring me can come into my life. The past is behind me, and so are the attitudes and ideas that go along with it. I'm a blessed child of yours, and from this day on I will treat myself and all those in my life and those who will be, as the always-changing, always-growing, loving creations of yours that we are. Thank you. Yes… Amen.

♥

> # *Those who've known you the longest aren't always those who know you the best*"

You give a lot of influence over your life to those you've known a long time.

It's as if the length of time you've known someone is the key that opens the door to your deepest emotions.

We dogs have a question for you.

Why do you give old friends and family so much power over how you feel?

What did they do to earn that influence, besides simply knowing you for a long time?

I inspired Bob to realize something powerful about this...

Those who've known you the longest aren't always those who know you the best.

In the time Bob and I have been together, Bob has revealed more of his personality to me than he's done to any human being he knows, family or friend.

And Bob loves his family and friends.

To Bob, I am pure love without judgment and, when you experience such divine perfect love like this in life, you find yourself opening up the depths of who you are and what you are in ways unlike anything you've ever done for anyone else.

The whole of you just wants to come out and express itself with such happiness and joy!

It's no wonder those in your people world will often say, *"I like dogs better than people."*

Like dogs, you've been created to be non-judgmental, to love unconditionally, and to accept anyone as they are, a child of God.

Just like we dogs love you.

And great friends do too.

That's one of the reasons why you feel such a closeness and bond with friends, many of whom you may only know for a brief time, more so than old friends and family you've been around for a long time.

The new friends don't know your history and couldn't care less about it.

You come to your new friends with a blank slate with nothing called *"My Past"* written on it.

Your new friends treat you unconditionally and accept you as who you are *today* and not as someone who is viewed by family and old friends who can never lose the years of prejudice and judgment in their eyes and hearts of what you were back *then*.

New friends do all of that for you because you do all of that for them.

Each of you wants to be accepted for the person you've *become* and not just as the person from where you came.

And don't you think that's the way God sees you too?

God doesn't care about your past.

Then *was so needed to get you to* now.

God took everything you experienced and has used it to teach you and help you become who you are, to get you to where you are and, most importantly, where you're on the way to going where God is going to take you.

Surround yourself with those who celebrate you.

Spend less time with those who simply tolerate you.

God is bringing the right people to you that you are looking for.

And when you meet them, you too will quickly realize…

Those who've known you the longest aren't always those who know you the best.

Dear God,

I am so blessed in so many ways. Thank you. I realize that everyone who is in my life is there for a reason and some will be in it only for a season. I let go of the expectation that someone else is supposed to make me happy or understand me. You make me happy, God. I make me happy by the thoughts I think, the dreams I have, and opening my heart and soul and mind to your guidance and direction. You created me. You know anything and everything about me, even all the things I've still yet to discover. Help me and take me to all that I can be. Let my life be a blessing to all who know, see, and hear about me. I'm so grateful and thankful to you, dear God. I love you. Thank you. Yes... Amen.

♥

> **When you look to others to fill your happiness tank, don't be surprised to find the fuel gauge always reading low"**

You humans sure love getting approval from others.

You believe they hold the keys to what you want and what you can be, so having them like you and what you do is a big thing.

Until they won't or don't.

It's like the world crashing down all around you.

"What about my dreams?"

"What about the things I want to have, be, or do?"

"What about how someone's disapproval is now going to make me feel?"

Wow… you sure do a number on yourselves.

And it's because you keep looking outside of yourself and to others to fill your happiness tank.

We dogs live our lives in a different way.

Let me tell you how living a life from your own approval and happiness is done.

Before I begin each new day, I never check in with Bob to let him know what I'm thinking of doing, how I'm thinking of doing it, why I'm doing it, and/or where I'll be doing it.

I just do it.

Because I *desire* to do it.

The only person (okay, dog) I get permission from is me.

Want to know why?

Because God calls me to do it.

One of the amazing things about how God works wonders in all of our lives is how the right people (and animals) are put into our lives at just the right time and for just the right reasons.

There's never any randomness.

There's never any chance.

There's never any coincidence.

It's all in perfect timing and for all the right reasons.

Take back your power.

God gave your life for *you* to live, and you don't need anyone else's approval or permission to do it.

Dear God,

thank you for awakening something inside of me that is inspiring me to live my life the way I want and desire. You created me and I'm a child of yours, and you give me all the direction, help, protection, blessings, and everything I can want or need to live the life of my dreams wherever you and those dreams and desires call me to. I let go of the opinions of others and choose to live from my own opinion, because nobody knows me, or my life, better than you and I. Thank you. Yes... Amen.

♥

> *Here's an easy way to know who to spend time with: Does that person spend more time talking about problems or possibilities?"*

Don't you just love being around people who make you feel good?

You remember their impact on you long after the conversation is over.

For good reason.

Those kinds of people are a rarity in your people world.

One that's filled with anxiety, fear, doubt, and worry.

It's easy to think you don't have too much choice in those you surround yourself with.

But you do.

In fact, *you're* the one who decides just who you'll let into your life and how long you'd like them to be there.

Bob loves spending time with me.

Every moment we're together is a joy, filled with overflowing happiness.

What's amazing is I love to talk to Bob with my bark, and I've never spoken a word.

And I'm always the pup he wants to hang out with!

My actions and how I live my life is only about possibilities and never about lack and limitation.

Just that experience alone has changed Bob's life for the best.

God has made it so easy for you to feel and be great, and a good place to start is by the company you keep.

Ask yourself this question: *Do the people in your life spend more time talking about problems or possibilities?*

The answer may surprise you.

Most of those in your people world don't realize the impact and influence others can have on your life.

We dogs do.

Start spending time with those who believe in you.

Start spending time with those who ask about you and truly care and want to know what's happening in your life.

Start spending time with those who encourage you and want to see you soar to greatness.

Once you sort everything out, you might be left with only a few true friends and family, but that's okay.

With the others being moved out of your life, God can now move the others, those who are good for you, and you good for them, into your life so that all of you will be blessings to each other.

Dear God,

thank you for showing me that I do have a choice in the people and family I choose to spend time with. I let go of the guilt and the feeling of obligation to anyone I know is not right for my divine, highest, best good. I release them with love and blessings and wish only the very best for them always. I so appreciate your bringing the right people, the best people, into my life, and me into theirs, so that we all can grow, experience, enjoy, and love this life and each other, and knowing that everything is divinely ordered, just the way you want it to be. You are my best friend, God. I love you. Thank you. Yes... Amen.

♥

> *You live in a world where there are more people who will tell you why you can't do something, than those who will tell you why you can. Find those who'll tell you why you can."*

We dogs are amazed at you humans.

We hear the words you say.

You know... those you tell yourself and others.

So why do so many of you think about and talk about the things that upset you, the things you don't want to happen, or the things that have happened that you just don't want to let go of?

And that's just the start.

Try finding those in your people world who have such a positive happy look on life, where they only want to talk about what *can* be and the good things they're looking forward to, and you will have quite a task ahead of you.

Oh, it wasn't always like that.

As a youngster, you came into this world happy and with so many dreams you couldn't contain them all.

Then those around you got to work.

Bit by bit, they squeezed that happiness right out of you, as they wrung out any dreams of yours *they* thought were too grand.

They did such a good job that you may have let yourself become one of them, just like so many do, where you now can easily talk about the things, problems, limitations, and frustrations that you can share with "friends."

We dogs call that "some friendship."

Bob considers himself blessed to have the two closest people (yes, that includes me, Cody!) in his life as the two most positive people he's ever known: Bob's mom and me.

When it comes to people, Bob's mom is the best friend he could have. She always looks on the positive and bright side of things and everyone loves her.

And talk about being 100 percent behind you!

One day, Bob can tell his mom that he's made a decision to move here or there and follow his dream and she will be thrilled.

The next day, Bob can tell her he's changed his mind and he's got a brand new plan, and she will be just as thrilled.

She is *always* focused on the *Why you can* and never on the *Why you can't*.

Then there's me, Cody.

Talk about my tail wiggling big time right now as I'm writing this!

Bob loves to tell people that I'm the best dog he could ever hope and pray for.

And every time he says that, my tail wiggles in happiness and joy!

Bob tells people that if I'm the only dog Bob will have in this lifetime, the love and experiences of having each other will be enough for 10 lifetimes.

And if you've ever loved a dog, Bob and I are willing to bet you can say the same too.

While I may not speak English, I do speak Doglish, and it's communicated by my actions, expressions, barks, and other sounds.

Bob loves talking to me every day, all throughout the day and night, and never ever do I or will I look at Bob with a scowl, unhappiness, frown, or disapproval whenever we talk about dreams, goals, and where and what we'd like to go to and do next.

The message I give to Bob is unmistakable: *"I'm your best friend in the world, and wherever you want to go and whatever you want to do whenever you want to do it, I'm always and forever 100 percent with you and by your side."*

God wants to you to have *those* kinds of people in your life.

You deserve nothing less.

And *they* deserve the blessing called *you*.

God gave you the power to think, the power to believe, and the power to choose who to *be* and who to be *with*.

If those you've been surrounding yourself with are less than inspiring and uplifting, it's time you let go and release whatever has been keeping them in your life.

Don't worry about how you'll let them go.

They'll slowly and *naturally* drift away, and as they do, God will introduce those who *are* good for you, and you good for them.

It may feel a bit uncomfortable at first, as you let go of what you've known and whom you've known for so long.

That's okay.

Take a leap of faith and just do it.

God knows how you feel and why you feel the way you do, and God knows what you need to make you feel brand new.

The kind of feeling you're going to experience when you surround yourself with people who will tell you about your possibilities.

You deserve nothing less.

Dear God,

for so long I've made compromises and have accepted people and things in my life that I knew deep down were not bringing me happiness. I know now that I don't have to accept anything less than only the things I want and desire because I deserve them. Dear God, I have so much to give to others. I have so much to give to myself and to this world that I'm so grateful to you I'm blessed to live in. Let me think and believe in a bigger and greater way, one I know I'm worthy of. Help me to let go of anyone and anything that keeps me from living in the happiness you've created me to live, love, and enjoy. Thank you for bringing the best people and experiences into my life that are in perfect harmony with my purpose you've created me to know and to live. This is a new day. This is fresh new beginning, and I'm so thankful to you for it all. I love you, God. Thank you. Yes... Amen.

♥

> *Choose carefully those you spend time with, for they will not let you rise any higher than what they are thinking, believing, or living without trying to make you feel guilty or an outcast"*

Many of you in your people world don't realize the power and influence other people have on you.

Especially if you work or go to school with them.

Your desire to be accepted in the relationship, group, or environment where you spend much of your time can be so powerful that, too often, you find yourself unhappy and can't quite put your finger on the reason why.

I can tell you why.

If you've got big dreams and desires, you're going to make those with little dreams and desires feel uncomfortable when they're around you.

Words of *"Why do you want to do that?"* are often said by those who'd like to keep you right where you are, so they can feel better about themselves' staying right where they are.

It's a good thing we dogs never spend much time hanging around those kinds of people.

Bob will tell you that I love being a maverick, as independent as they come.

I love exploring the new, the untried, and the unknown.

It's the kind of life God speaks to me to go to and live, and I always go because *I'm being called to it.*

Imagine if you lived your life more like we dogs do.

You'd love and respect anyone and everyone, yet you'd love them enough to not be interested in listening to any talk of staying *where* you are and staying *who* you are.

You're being called to go and to grow.

Like us dogs, you're connected to the wisest and greatest power in the world that is guiding your every step, every dream, every desire, and every result.

God will never speak lack and limitation into your life.

God will only remind you of what's possible.

God will never try and hold you back from rising up and becoming bigger and better.

God will only remind you that anything you dream of and believe, you can have.

Listen less to others and more to the divine voice from within, and your life will begin to amaze you.

Dear God,

thank you for bringing into my life the right people who will be my true friends and will know, understand, encourage, and inspire me to a greater, bigger, happier, and more joyful and fulfilling inspired life. Thank you for helping and showing me how to do the same for them. I bless all the family and friends who are and have been in my life, and I want only the very best for them. I release anyone and anything from my life that keeps me from doing your will. You created me for your purpose, and I want to live it and love it. You are with me always, and I am with you always. Together we are the best for each other. I love you, God. Thank you. Yes... Amen.

♥

> ## Let go of who and what's not ready for you, so that those who are and that which is can come into your life"

Many of those in your people world live from a belief of lack and limitation and that there's not enough of anything in the world you live in.

You hold on to the past, whether it's old acquaintances that are negative draining influences or stuff that's more upkeep than enjoyment, and you keep holding onto them from the belief of lack and limitation.

I'm going to let you in on a secret.

It's one we dogs know so very well…

There is always enough.

Not only enough, but an *overabundance of enough* of anything you could ever desire.

As dogs, our connection to God is pure and always flowing.

One of the things we know is that in your world, *you can have anything your heart and soul desires, and not only will you get what you believe, you'll get far more than you expect and can conceive.*

God made it so beautifully that way.

Look at the miracle of Nature.

Just one kernel seed of corn can produce hundreds more seeds of corn.

When Nature makes a new plant, Nature doesn't make just one plant, but an *overabundance* of them.

When God makes a fish, God makes not just one fish egg, but *hundreds* of them.

God knows nothing of lack and limitation.

Those come from your people-created beliefs.

And if you've been living your life for far too many years by such beliefs, I have something to tell you...

Let things go and let people go who are not supposed to be in your life any longer.

You can never receive the next best thing as long as you keep holding on to the same old thing.

Everything in your life is happening in divine perfect timing.

Everything.

You stay in others' lives and they stay in yours for just the right time and for just the right reasons.

And once you've learned from them and they've learned from you, then it's time for you and them to move forward to the next great God-inspired experience each of you is being called to.

God knows exactly where you are at this moment.

And God knows where and how and when God is going to take you to the next great moment.

This is a new day.

It's time let go of who and what's not ready for you so that those who are and that which is can come into your life.

Dear God,

this is going to be the day when I let go. Let go of the old beliefs and the old ways of thinking and doing things. I bless them all, for I know they've all helped get me to the place where I am at this moment. I am so ready for a new beginning, a fresh new start and brand new chance to begin something new in my life. As I let the old past and its ways go, I open every door to you, dear God, to flood and overflow my life with your blessings, abundance, love, and experiences that I can feel deep inside of me that you're calling me to. Take this blessed life of mine that I'm so grateful and thankful for and make me, and it, into everything you know and want it to be. I'm ready and I'm yours, dear God. I love you with everything inside my heart and soul. Thank you. Yes… Amen.

♥

> ## *Spend more time with those who celebrate you and less time with those who tolerate you"*

Have you ever told someone who really doesn't know you, about some of the good things that are happening in your life?

What was their enthusiasm and happiness like upon hearing such news?

Was it greater than you've ever received from family or old friends?

It happens to those in your people world all the time.

It can be a rarity in this life to find old friends and family who truly celebrate your success without their feeling uneasy about it.

Your moving forward is a reminder of their staying still.

Where you're on the way to going is a reminder of where they're on the way to remaining.

For you the sky is the limit, and for them life is full of limits.

Imagine how happy it must make God feel when you're around people who celebrate you and you celebrate them.

If there is one creature that truly embodies the best of the kind of family and friends you can hope for, it's a dog.

And for Bob, that dog is me, the happy boy named Cody.

It can be the tiniest of successes, like *"Hey Cody, I just played on my guitar one of the songs I wrote in a different way!"* and I'll be so excited and want to celebrate it, that it's just like we had won the biggest lottery prize in history!

Big or small, it's equally important for Bob and me to celebrate them all.

Why?

Because I always look at Bob the way God looks at Bob.

It's the same way God sees you.

Every moment is the perfect moment for us to celebrate ourselves and each other.

Our life is a gift.

Our life is a miracle.

Our life is a blessing.

Our life comes from God, who lives in us as us.

And we are God-worthy of every good thing we dream of or desire, and of everything we do.

Spend more time with those who celebrate you and less time with those who tolerate you.

And when you do, you'll always be finding new and wonderful things to celebrate with each other.

Dear God,

I celebrate this moment when I'm thinking about you and how truly, incredibly blessed I am. Thank you! I love you and I love me. Thank you for bringing into my life the right people for the right reasons. Thank you for all of us being inspirations to each other. I'm so grateful to have people in my life who love, support, and encourage me, and I love doing the same for them. Friends are one of your greatest gifts that I can experience in this blessed life, and I thank you for every one of them. I ask that you bless all of us in every way, as we live our lives to the dreams you are calling us to. Let me be your hands and feet and let my actions and words help make your other children's lives better, happier, more joyful, and touched by our love. Thank you. Yes... Amen.

♥

> *Blessed be those who ask you about and remind you of the things that are your passions, dreams, and desires"*

The timing of the perfectly asked question or inspiring word.

You all need it.

You all want it.

Not often enough do you get it.

Not even from those you call family and friends.

People are so busy being distracted by the things they hold in their hands and look at, that they rarely think about anything or anyone else.

You've met them.

You might have lots of them you call friends.

Those who, when you talk to them, speak so much about themselves and rarely, if ever, ask a question about you.

Thank goodness we dogs don't do that or have things that distract us.

If you ask Bob, he'll happily tell you that I've spoiled him.

In the best of ways.

Every moment of every day, I'm 100 percent focused on Bob.

Without even speaking a word of English (I speak Doglish instead!), I can sense and read Bob's mannerisms, words, and the sound and tone of his voice.

I watch every move Bob makes and is about to make.

I know what Bob is thinking without his saying a word, and each and every time I'm right.

When Bob does say a word, my actions are just the perfect thing Bob needs at the perfect time.

Parents and those who love you are like that.

They, especially moms, know you better than anyone else.

One of the gifts a parent gives you is that they'll ask you and speak to you about things they know that are important to you, the things you want, and those things they know would make you happy.

Just the simplest of questions at the time you need to hear them can *shift* your thinking.

Like the time Bob was talking to his mom.

I'll often hear Bob talking to his mom on the phone and telling her about where we're currently living and the things he's so busy doing there, and then unexpectedly she'll ask, "Do you like it there?"

Such a simple question.

And one that made him stop for a moment and think if he *really* did like being where we were.

Turns out, he knew it, she knew it, and I knew it, that we were ready to move and go to the next great place in our Cody & Bob Adventure.

Those are the kinds of words, spoken at just the perfect time you need to hear them, that God inspires others to speak to you.

Words that can lift you out of your rut or get you thinking in a fresh new way and direction that can change your life.

Here's something fun to try.

Next time you're with or speaking with a friend, ask God that your thoughts and words be divinely inspired and try going beyond yourself and step into *their* world for just a moment.

Ask them about their life, what they're doing, and what they're thinking of doing, and encourage them.

Keep asking and keep listening until they are done talking to you about the things that matter to them right now in their lives.

So many in your people world are starved for attention and to have those in their lives who care about them.

And when you do, you're about to make a *big* difference in your life and in that person's life.

Dear God,

one of the things I've learned in this life is that you created people for each other. We are meant to love and care for one another like we do for ourselves. So many times, I get so involved and self-absorbed in my own world that I don't give friends, family, and others the love and attention I know I could give if I really wanted to. Help me to change that, dear God. You created me for a purpose higher and greater than myself, and one in which I can help and inspire others. To give this world and the people in it my gifts, talents, and abilities that you have so lovingly blessed me with so I can help make their lives better in some way. Show me all the gifts, talents, and abilities you've blessed me with, and teach me how to use them to fullest of my God-given abilities. Open every door for us so that I can take who and what you've created me to be, to make this world, its people, and my life, the best that it can be. Thank you so much, dear God. I love you. Thank you. Yes... Amen.

♥

Blessings shared are blessings doubled"

Have you ever received blessings and good news in your life?

Have you ever just kept those blessings and good news to yourself?

How did it feel?

How about when you shared those blessings and good news with others?

How did it feel?

Way different, right?

When you share your blessings and good news with others, the good news and blessings feel increased.

And they become increased by your belief and attention to them.

When you share the things with others you've *let* upset you, isn't amazing how those burdens just feel like they've been cut in half or melted away and gone altogether?

Bob loves to tell people that I'm his precious and priceless blessing from God in so many ways.

And Bob is mine!

One of the ways is that I'm Bob's best friend to whom he can talk about any and everything.

He can talk to me about his deepest desires, feelings, and thoughts, always knowing I'm listening, loving, and caring for as long and as often as Bob wants to talk to me.

Bob can talk to me about things he never talks to anyone else about, especially at the moments when those thoughts and feelings are fresh, new, raw, vulnerable, and otherwise would be open to judgment from even people Bob deeply loves and those who love him.

I never judge.

I never will.

I never can.

I'm God's pure bundle of unconditional love that's come to this earth to be with Bob as a dog.

The best dog and best friend Bob could ever hope or pray for.

Your dog, if you have one or you've ever had one, is *the same* for you.

And your dog, when you *will* have one, will be *the same* for you.

If you'll let God open your heart and soul and receive *all* that's been and being created for you to experience and enjoy by having *"your dog"* in your life.

The quickest and best friend for life (this one and all the others that will follow) is when you bring one of us home.

And once you do, *you will never be alone.*

Ever.

Dear God,

I let go of thinking I need to know it all, do it all, keep it all, and not share the things in my life with those I love and those who love me. Thank you for bringing into my life the right people, animals, and anything else at the right time for the right reasons. Thank you for inspiring me to share my life with those you've put into my life at this moment for your divine perfect reasons, and for them to share theirs with me. Help me to inspire and love them and let me let them love and inspire me as we all lift each other to lives of higher and greater joy, purpose, and love. Thank you. Yes... Amen.

♥

> ## *Spend less time on things to buy and more time on things to love"*

Stuff.

You've just got to have it.

You spend hours thinking about it, searching for it, buying it, waiting for it, using it, and then getting tired of it so you can get rid of it.

Only to find yourself back in the place where…

You can't wait to spend the money you don't have to buy more of the things you don't need.

It never ends.

Dogs don't care about stuff.

Bob will tell you I don't have a wallet or a bank account, yet I'm the richest living creature he knows.

My wealth is unlimited.

My wealth knows no bounds.

My riches come from God, and they're always in the currency of love.

Bob and I love having nice things.

We love the homes and places where we live, and we thank God every day for our blessings.

We know that while "stuff" is great to want, to have, and to enjoy, real joy and happiness will never be found in the having.

It's only in the giving.

The giving of ourselves to be kind and loving to people and animals everywhere we go.

The giving of ourselves by always being happy, positive, optimistic, enthusiastic, fun, joyful, inspiring, and encouraging to everyone we know and to anyone we will meet.

The giving of our love and affection anywhere at anytime to whoever needs it, and listening to God's inspiration and direction to find them and then touch their lives in some way for the better.

Bob and I don't get up every day and have to think, "*Just who are we going to meet today, where will we meet them, and what will we say to them?*"

Life takes care of all the details of the who, the where, the when, the why, and the how.

Bob and I don't know all the reasons *why* we are getting this calling.

We just know we are.

And we don't care *where* the calling to give love is taking us.

Our lives began to change in the most amazing of ways when we began living our lives more from the place of…

We trust you God, you created us for you and to touch the lives of your children and animals and in some way make them better, and we're going to have faith and trust and follow your guidance and inspiration to do so, wherever it takes us.

God created and inspires me to live my life that way, and I show and inspire Bob to do the same.

Think back to any experience you've ever had in your life, and you will find something that has never changed.

One of the greatest joys you ever felt was when you made a positive difference in someone else's life.

And I'll go further…

The difference you made in that person's life helped change that person's life in ways you will never know.

You have *that* much power.

God has made it easy for you to experience the greatest, deepest, and most lasting joy in your life.

And it all begins by doing one thing.

Spend less time on things to buy and more time on things to love.

Dear God,

I'm so grateful for your teaching me that a life helping and inspiring others is a life unmatched in happiness, and fulfillment by anything else. You created everyone for each other, and I thank you for that. Help me to make a positive difference in someone's life each day. Help me to be humble and let someone else make a difference in my life each day too. I humble myself and know that each person you've created is loved and cared for equally by you. Thank you for opening my eyes, heart, and soul to see everyone I share this planet with as my brothers and sisters. I love them. I love me. I love you, dear God. Thank you. Yes… Amen.

♥

I came here to love"

We dogs know something that can change your life.

And if you'll let the power, presence and meaning of what I'm about to tell you sink in deep inside of you, it will so change your thinking and life, you'll wish you had a tail like ours that you could wiggle.

You came here to love.

You came into this world to give yourself away.

To love this life, your life, and everything and everyone in it.

New things to buy get old.

Love never does.

New travels and experiences are more exciting to plan and look forward to than the actual experience of them.

Love is always fresh and renewed with never a limit or ending to be found.

Think of what it means to be a dog.

We are pure divine love with fur, paws, and tails that wiggle with joy and happiness.

As Bob likes to say to me, "You're my love bundle."

We love life, and we want to give all that is us to someone else.

And we wake up each day so excited to do it again and again, and we never count the cost.

That's what it feels like to be one of us.

The greatest joy and happiness you will ever know and can ever know in this life is when you live in love and give *all* that you are to the world.

And let the world love you too.

As the giver *and* receiver.

You are worthy of the greatest joys and love anyone can ever know.

And you have proof of it every second of every day.

God loves *you* so much that God created you so you could *know* what love *feels* like.

Share it and change someone's life by it.

That's when you'll know how love is *lived*.

Dear God,

I am so grateful for my life and the gift of this new day. I came here for a mighty purpose, and one of my life's purposes is to love and help others. Show me how to use every gift, talent, and ability that you've so lovingly blessed me with, to really make a difference in the lives of my brothers and sisters who are your children. I want to help people, inspire them, and make their lives better. Inspire me and show me how to live my life with purpose and passion and to give love and keep giving love as you endlessly fill the love in my heart and soul for myself and to share with every soul I may touch by it. Thank you, God. I love you. Thank you. Yes… Amen.

♥

The right relationships are always easy"

How many times have you heard or read that you have to work hard at having a good relationship?

Really?

Do you believe it?

Who convinced you of such a thing?

Think about a best friend.

How hard do you have to work or much have you had to give up, to have a best friend and to keep one?

I'll bet you say, *"Very little, if anything."*

That's because the *right* relationship is easy.

Bob will tell you that I'm the best friend he's ever known, and never once does it seem like work to him or to me, being the two best friends in the world.

It feels like the most perfect and natural thing in the world for us to do and for us to be.

You see, when it comes to relationships, one word makes all the difference…

Right.

The *right* relationship.

That's what you want, and that's the one worth waiting for, no matter how long it takes to arrive to you.

And it will.

Just let God bring it you.

So what does the *right* relationship feel like?

The *right* relationship is *easy*.

The *right* relationship is *fun*.

The *right* relationship is *natural*.

The *right* relationship is *inspiring*.

The *right* relationship awakens all the good that's inside of you.

The *right* relationship is always changing and growing into something more, something better, deeper, and more meaningful.

The *right* relationship feels purposeful, true, genuine, relaxed, and meant to be, like your favorite sweatshirt and shoes you always want to put on because they just feel *so* good.

That's the *right* relationship!

You deserve nothing less.

Dear God,

it's so good to know that I don't have to settle for less or second best, or to compromise on what I truly want. I can have any and all of the desires of my heart. I thank you for bringing into my life the best people for the right reasons at just the perfect times for them to be in my life and me to be in theirs. I'm your child. I deserve the most wonderful people and experiences, and I open my belief to allow them in without exception or limitation. The good, the joy, happiness, love, prosperity, abundance, and blessings I can receive are unlimited because you are unlimited. I'm your blessed creation and child. I take all the limits off of you, dear God. I thank you for the truly incredible things you are doing and are about to do in every part of my life. Day by day, in every way, I am getting better and better and more blessed. I love you. Thank you. Yes... Amen.

♥

4

LOVING YOURSELF
AND THE GIFT CALLED
YOUR LIFE

When you look at yourself, you're looking at God"

How rarely do you let it sink in that you are made in the image of God.

From my eyes, when I look at Bob, I see him as perfect, whole, and complete.

These are the same eyes that look at us through the divine eyes of innocence, purity and perfection by The One who created all of us—God.

Look at the divine perfection and innocence of a baby.

In so many ways, dogs and babies are just alike.

A blank canvas of only love and good things until others teach them fears, worries, doubts, anxieties, insecurities, and phobias.

Yet, the perfection of that baby you once were is always there inside of you, waiting to be released again.

Let yourself see yourself through the eyes of God once again.

You are and will always be God's perfect creation.

Dear God,

I am so grateful for this day, this moment, and the gift of life you have given to me. Help me to see me as you see me, as a child of yours and one who is divinely created and worthy of every blessing and joy from you. Show me that as I see the divinity that's me, I will also see that same divinity in everyone and everything you have created. Thank you. Yes... Amen.

♥

Many have forgotten that from God they are begotten"

Everything you own is made by someone somewhere, and having it makes your life better simply by its use.

Bob loves knowing that I'm his every-day-I-look-at-you living proof that he, you, I, and everything and everyone else in this world, is made by the greatest maker of all, God.

The more Bob looks and watches me live, move, and have my being on this earth with him, the more he realizes just how amazing that he, you, and everyone else have been created too.

God didn't get anything wrong when God made us.

Dogs and people are divine living and breathing perfections in every way.

All of us look the way we do, have the personalities we have, act the way we act, and dream the way we dream, because we are made for a purpose.

God desires to live through you in this moment and experience with you only the things you can experience in only the ways you can experience them.

Think of the power and importance of this.

God created you so God could live through you as you.

Dear God,

thank you for this moment to talk to you. In my busy life, I sometimes think about it, yet so often I do not take the time to stop, breathe, think, and be truly grateful for this gift of life you have so lovingly blessed me with. I am so thankful that you created me. I thank you for all the people, animals, and everything in my life—past, present and future—because it all comes from you. Thank you for reminding me each and every day, just how amazing you've created me to be in every way. I love you. Thank you. Yes... Amen.

♥

Love always finds you when you let go"

Why is it that when you don't have something in your life and you keep thinking about what you don't have, it seems like it takes forever for what you want to make its way to you?

Then, when you get it, even *more* of it keeps showing up in your experiences and life.

Funny how that works, isn't it?

I taught Bob the wonderful lesson of why.

Bob always gives me the complete freedom to live my life how I want, without Bob smothering me or wanting to control me.

And do you know what I choose?

To always be next to Bob and live it with him.

My unspoken message to Bob is…

"Love always finds you when you let go."

God has designed our world the same way.

Keep your mind off of the lack and unhappiness of it and instead on the desire and belief of it, and watch how more of what you focus on keeps coming into your life.

Imagine and feel yourself *already* living and loving the life and those you desire to be in it, and then release the need of control to know the how, when, who, and where.

Once you do, you can be assured *love always finds you when you let go.*

Dear God,

you've made everything in this life so simple. Let go of the need for control and let people and things go and let them come back to you in their own divinely perfect way and time. It's taken many years for me to realize this and, now that I do, I cannot even begin to tell you how much happier I feel and my life is. Thank you, God, for showing that to me. Yes, from this day on, I will be the giver of love to any and everyone I meet. And I know what will happen when I do. The more I give love, the more love will be returned to me. Dear God, it's true. I love life and life loves me. Thank you for loving me. I love you, dear God. Thank you. Yes... Amen.

♥

> *Start being good to yourself*
> *again and let yourself*
> *enjoy the masterfully*
> *choreographed play of how*
> *your life unfolds each day"*

Those in your people world make their lives so much harder than they need to be.

Who needs enemies when the worst one you'll ever face is yourself?

Why you are so tough and demanding on yourself?

Where did you learn to do such a thing, and why do you keep doing *anything* that brings you unhappiness?

We dogs know the answer.

Somewhere along your life's road, you picked up the belief that you're unworthy of great things and a life of ease and happiness.

So you've kept living with the belief that supports that by being too critical, too tough, too demanding, and too unforgiving on yourself and others.

Please… give that stuff up.

It's time to start being good to yourself again.

Can I tell you a secret?

I have it from divine authority that nowhere is it written in your life's manual that the tougher you are on yourself, the greater the reward you'll receive—*either in the here or the after.*

Every moment of every day is God's gift to you.

You are created as pure love, and when you're anything other than that, you feel unhappy.

As a dog, I live my life differently.

I'm *always* good to myself.

Never in my life has there been, nor will there ever be, a day or a time where I'll beat myself up over anything.

Just imagine how good you'd feel if you had just *one* of those days or weeks where you never criticize or judge yourself or others?

Just how wonderful do you think that would feel?

I can tell you.

It's going to feel wonderful and so perfectly *natural* because that's who God created you to be.

Say *"Goodbye"* to your inner critic.

Say *"Hello"* to a kinder and more loving you.

The one that's going to show you what real happiness is all about.

Dear God,

thank you for showing me how to be my own best friend. Thank you for filling me with your peace, presence, and love and inspiring within me how it feels to be divinely loved by you. I let go of being the critic of my life and anyone else's. I let go of being so demanding, impatient, unkind, and judgmental about anyone and anything. I'm so grateful for your understanding, patience, love, hope, faith and belief in me, your child, who loves you. You and I are one, dear God. I ask you to guide every area of my life, for I give it all to you. Thank you. Yes… Amen.

♥

5

YOU'VE BEEN CREATED FOR A GREAT PURPOSE

> ## *You are here because God desires to live and to experience this life, right now, through you, as you*"

Perhaps the greatest question you can ask yourself is *"Why am I here?"*

Deep within each of you is the insatiable desire to know your purpose, the *"why"* of why you were created.

When you were kids, you were so much like us dogs!

You couldn't have cared less about asking such a question because the only thing you cared about was having fun.

Then things changed.

As you got older, you were taught to give up your childish ways and that life is difficult and fraught with problems to always get over, only to make room for the next problem on the way.

Then you did *the adult things* like getting married, having kids, buying a house, cars, and the other stuff you're *supposed* to have and enjoy.

Yet, as the years have gone by, faster and faster, always in the back of your mind has lingered *that* question…

"Why am I here?"

Can I let you in on a secret?

I know the answer.

Because God desires to live and to experience this life, right now, through you, as you.

Think about that.

God created you, with your never-to-be-repeated-or-found-in-anyone-else personality, looks, talents, abilities, dreams, and desires, so that *God could live as God in you, through you, and as you.*

The answer to *why* you're here has been found.

And it's been inside of you your whole life.

As a dog, I know just how amazing and special I am.

No other animal ever *looks* like me.

No other animal ever *acts* like me.

No other animal ever *understands* like me.

No other animal ever *loves* like me.

No other animal will ever *be* like me.

And you can say the same.

Dear God,

I so appreciate you and knowing, truly knowing, that you created me for you so that we could experience all the joys and happiness of my life, in this life, together as one. Thank you so much. I want you to show me how I can let you make my life the most wonderful life it can possibly be. I take the limits off of you, dear God, for all the things you desire to do in my life. I want to touch people's lives in only positive, loving, and empowering ways. Help me to let go of anything and everything that keeps me from experiencing and enjoying the fullness of your blessings. We are one. I love you dear God. Thank you. Yes… Amen.

♥

> # *If God gave you life, don't you think God can also give you direction?"*

Those in your people world take so many things for granted.

Like the air you breathe.

You rarely think about it because you expect it to always be there when you want it.

It's the same for your life.

You've been here in your body as who you are for so long, that you just take it for granted you'll wake up to another day.

And what a blessing and miracle that new day is, and so are all the possibilities in it, just waiting to be discovered!

Yet, for many of you, those blessings and possibilities remain undiscovered.

You wake up to another day of doing pretty much what you've always done, and later that evening, you'll go to bed so you can get up and do it all again tomorrow.

It doesn't have to be like that.

Bob will tell you that waking up with me and watching me live my happy life each and every day is a gift to him beyond measure.

For me too!

Each new day is like every holiday you could name and a birthday and New Year's all in one!

And every day is like that, from the time I was just a puppy to this day that I'm loving and living my life.

Every day, and all throughout it, I'm connected to God and listening to God giving me inspiration that takes me to the next fun thing to do and the next.

It just never stops.

As Bob began being more like me and living his life more like the way I am, Bob started to notice something very interesting happening within him.

Not only is he happier—though if you ask people who know him, they'll tell you Bob's always been a happy boy—Bob started to feel the pressures of needing to "figure it out" being lifted from his life because he was trusting God more and more to take care of it and direct every part of it.

As Bob does so, a powerful inspiring truth has slowly begun to sink in…

If God gave you life, don't you think God can also give you direction?

Bob and I know the answer.

Now you will too.

Dear God,

something very powerful is happening in my life. Now that I look in the mirror, I don't just see the person I am. I see you in me as me. We are one. You are the one who created me. You are the one who keeps me in perfect wellbeing and always will. You are the one who protects me. You are the one who guides me. You are the one who inspires me. You are the one from where all of my blessings come. And you and I are one, created and living and loving this life for each other. I am so grateful, thankful and appreciative for anything and everything, dear God. I'm so happy and excited to be living this moment and this day. I cannot wait for tomorrow because we are going to experience brand new things in brand new ways. Thank you for your goodness, your love, and all of your blessings. Thank you for helping me to use every gift, talent, and ability you've so lovingly blessed me with so that we can touch people's lives in such loving, divinely inspired and amazing ways. I love you God. I am yours, dear God. Thank you. Yes… Amen.

♥

> *You created me to be great,*
> *and you gave me the desire*
> *to experience it"*

Everything about you says one thing...

Greatness.

You were created to be great.

Greater than you've ever allowed yourself to be.

You always know when you keep yourself from the good God wants to give you and the greatness God wants you to become.

It feels *empty.*

It feels *less than.*

It feels like there's something *missing.*

It feels like there needs to be *more.*

Lots more.

And there is.

Each day Bob and I are blessed to be with each other, I love to show Bob things he can never learn from another person or himself.

Things God wants me to *show* Bob.

Things God wants me to *teach* Bob.

Things God wants me to *inspire* Bob.

And do I ever.

Every moment of every day, I live and love my life with everything I am.

I never stop at the destination called "Good Enough."

For me, only *"This is great"* will do.

Like Bob and me, God created you to be great.

Yet God didn't stop at great.

God gave you the desire to experience it.

It's when you don't or won't let yourself experience your greatness that you keep your blessings from arriving in your life.

Think of the power of our creator.

God is everywhere, in everyone, and in everything all at the same time.

It's astonishing to think of such power and the all-that-is-ness of that.

Everything God does is great.

Everything God will ever create is great.

And that greatness is on the inside of you.

Today is the day you are going to begin letting it out.

Dear God,

I hear you calling me forward to release the greatness inside of me. Thank you for inspiring me to be bigger, better, happier, more joyful and to let myself feel the greatness of whom I am and follow your calling wherever you guide me. I let go of the old way of thinking, believing, and experiencing. I am your child; a living, sacred, blessed and miraculous creation filled with everything you are. Thank you for reminding me that I deserve the greatness you have placed inside of me along with all the happiness and joys to experience it. I will never stop listening to you dear God. I love you with all my heart and soul. Thank you. Yes... Amen.

♥

6

THE POWER
OF FAITH TO CHANGE
YOUR LIFE

Inside of you is a voice that is always calling you to change"

No matter your age, no matter where you live, no matter who you are and what you do, inside of you is a voice that's always calling you to change.

The voice never stops.

Nor will it.

It is God talking to you.

Many of you try and ignore it.

The wisest of you listen and follow it.

Bob will tell you I'm one of them.

As I look back on all the years Bob and I have been blessed to be together, we have both had front row seats to watch all the changes each of us has been living.

We are living them together in real time, and it's thrilling.

One year, we can be living in one state and town and just having the most fun two best buddies can have, and the next year, we are so ready to move that we get so excited just counting down the days and hours until it happens.

What's happening?

God is *changing* us.

God is *calling* us.

And we *listen*.

Right now, there are many things you'd like to change in your life.

Right now, there are many dreams and goals you'd like to see become a reality.

Right now, there are many things you'd like to have, be, do, and experience that you're not letting yourself have and enjoy.

Right now, *God is calling you to them.*

The question is: Will you let yourself go to them?

If fear, doubt, and worry are answering the question, the answer will always be "No."

If faith, trust, and belief are answering the question, the answer will always be "Yes."

Listen to your "Yes."

God wants to begin a great work in you that's about to bring you joy and happiness like you've never known.

Dear God,

I'm so grateful for this day and every day you bless me with. When I was younger, I had so many dreams that made me so happy just thinking about them. As the years have gone by, I know I've let the expectations of life, from others and from myself, push my dreams far back so I won't have to think about them. Yet, all my life, I've known they're still there. They've always been there. They'll always be there because they come from you, dear God. You know better than I or anyone else what it is I love to do, what it is I dream to do, and what it is you know I was created to do. I don't care about my age or anything else. I'm ready to live my dreams. I'm ready for you to take me to every blessing and experience you desire for me. I am here to do your will, dear God. Now I'm ready for you to open all the doors and show me how to do it. I love you, God. Thank you. Yes... Amen.

♥

The four words that can change your life: "Talk to me, God'"

Imagine if someone told you that by saying four words and truly meaning them, your life could begin to change in ways you would like.

I know it in ways only we dogs can.

I love being outside.

I love feeling the warmth of the sunshine all over my body and feeling the fresh air kiss me with every breeze that blows.

As I make my way around the perimeter of our yard, I love to just stop, put my head in the air, look at the sky, and take a deep *thankful* breath that says, *"Talk to me, God,"* and then move my paws in the direction the inspiration within leads me.

That inspiration guides me.

Perfectly.

Every single time.

God wants to do the same for you.

All God needs is an invitation from you to let God know you are ready to listen to God's divine guidance for you.

Tonight, step outside just for moment.

Look at the sky above you and the amazing universe that surrounds you.

Breathe in and then whisper these words that can change your life…

Dear God,

thank you for this great day. I know you have made me for a purpose greater than that which I've let myself become. I desire to do more, to be more, and to become more. Talk to me, God. Inspire me and show me the right way to go. Thank you for helping me to be who and all you created me to be. Thank you. Yes... Amen.

♥

> ## *God doesn't care what you call God... God just wants you to call"*

Those in your people world get so hung up on names.

They place so much importance on feeling good about what they call things and making sure what they call them is categorized in the right place.

Like God.

As long as humans have lived on this earth, they've called God all sorts of names.

As Bob has watched and lived with me all these years, something interesting began to intrigue Bob...

How could I, Bob's dog, Cody, have the full *God-Always-On Experience* in my life, if I never went to a house of prayer, house of worship, participated in a religious ceremony or rite of passage, or uttered words those in your people world are told they must say before they can ever know or have access to the God who created them?

Here I am, a dog that, every moment of every day, is a four-legged living, moving, and breathing expression of the love of God more than any human so many in your people world will ever know.

Day after day, year after year, as Bob watches me, this divinely inspired creation from God named Cody, the answer of *how* and *why* becomes clear...

I never forget who I am and who created me.

The Cody-to-God and God-to-Cody connection is *always* on.

I never need to think about what to call God because I'm *always* calling God.

Give yourself a break.

We dogs want you to know something.

God doesn't care what you call God.

God just wants you to call.

From the moment I was born to the moment I'll close my eyes and make my return back into God's spirit, *I'll never stop calling God.*

Think of how amazing your life can be if only you'll do more of the same.

Dear God,

your love, power, and presence in my life is unlike anything I'll ever experience from anyone or anything else. I want you to be number one in my life, and I ask that each day you show me how to live my life from your divine blessings and inspiration. I'm so grateful, thankful and appreciative for it all. You are incredible. I am incredible, and together we are a power unlike anything in this world. Thank you. Yes... Amen.

♥

> ## *There are unlimited ways to get from where you are to where you next want to go"*

You like knowing what's ahead.

You like knowing you've got things figured out when it comes to what you're going to do next with your life.

Many times, the path you *plan* to travel along turns out not to be the one you actually *do* travel on.

That unexpected path is the God path.

And when many of you experience it, because it didn't come from you, you question whether it's the right path.

Smile.

It *always* is.

In the divinely inspired world of a dog, there's no stopping when it's time to go after something you want.

You take a step, and then another step, then another step and another step, and you keep taking those steps *until* you reach what you want or something even better.

Rarely will all your steps be in a straight line to where you're going.

If you're on the divine path, you don't even care if they are.

You're connected to the power and wisdom that created you and guides you and wants to show you…

There are unlimited ways to get from where you are to where you next want to go.

The toughest thing for many of you to do is to trust anyone or anything outside of yourself.

Especially when it comes to the direction of your life.

Yet, when you begin to trust God more, you begin trusting yourself more at the same time.

So how on this earth could you ever go wrong?

You can't.

And you won't.

Be more like my dog buddies and me.

Know what you want.

Believe you can have it.

Trust God to take you to it.

And God always will… or to something even better.

Dear God,

I am so grateful to you for this day and all my blessings. Thank you. What joy there is to know that I don't have to figure it all out to get to where I want and to have what I dream and desire. You are my guide, and I trust you to take me to all the blessings you want me to have and to enjoy. Thank you for being so good to me. Inspire me in ways only you can. Guide me in ways only you know. Help me in ways that come only from you so that I may do your will and follow that will and the life you've created for me wherever you and it take me. Thank you. Yes... Amen.

♥

We'll lead... you follow"

Ever wonder why we dogs want to lead whenever we're being walked?

I can tell you.

Because God is calling us to all the good stuff, and we know just where it is.

Oh yes...

If only you'd let us guide you to it.

Instead, you pull back on the leash because you believe you know better what's best for dogs.

Sounds kinda like your life.

Nice try.

I love inspiring Bob about letting the next inspiration lead you to the next inspiration.

You'll only know the way all us dogs know which way to go, when you let yourself trust God for your direction and life like we do.

Here's something to think about the next time you see someone else walking a dog.

We dogs are not reading maps or watching a listening to a GPS or app telling us where to go.

We are all eyes, ears, and nose.

We live by *instinct and inspiration.*

Instinct and inspiration placed inside of us by God.

The *same* instinct inside of you right now that's all loaded, set, and ready to go.

Instinct that's ready to guide, propel, protect, encourage, and bless you.

The only question is…

When will you let it?

Dear God,

I'm so thankful that I have you in control of every part of my life. You know every road, every person, every experience I will travel along and have, and the best way to take me from where I am to where I desire to be. I let go of the need to be in control of every detail of my life. You created me. You know me better than I know myself. I gladly give you the reins to my life and ask you to guide, protect, and bless it in your divinely perfect way. Yes God, you lead and I'll happily follow. Thank you. Yes… Amen.

> *There's nothing you cannot have that you have not kept away from yourself. Ask yourself 'Why?' and the answer will change your life.*

Imagine someone sitting down with you.

Someone who knows you even better than you do.

Imagine this person showing you something you've never seen before.

Your potential.

Your potential for *happiness.*

Your potential for *love.*

Your potential for *greatness.*

You look stunned.

Never before have you seen these things.

Never before have you known these things.

To that person you ask, *"Why haven't I lived these things?"*

And from them you hear...

"Because you don't believe."

That someone is God.

God is talking to is *you.*

Can I tell you a secret?

I've never had that conversation with God before I came to this earth to be with Bob as a dog named Cody.

I didn't have to.

I know from where and whom I come.

I *instinctively* know God has guaranteed my greatness and happiness.

All I need to do is allow it to pour forth from within by living the life I *desire*.

You have *that* kind of greatness on the inside of you right now.

You've *always* had it inside of you.

Your *belief* in yourself and God is what lets it out.

Your *faith* in God and in yourself has given you the life you have lived.

And it's how *worthy* you feel in deserving to be greater, that keeps giving you the life you're now living, that which you'll live tomorrow, and for all the days that follow.

Time and time again, just when Bob thinks I've showed him all I'm capable of, be it love, happiness or anything else, I'll reach down inside of me and into that inexhaustible storehouse of greatness from God and I become *more*.

So much more.

You have that *same* inexhaustible storehouse of greatness inside of you.

You have the unlimited power and potential to have, be, and do *anything* you'll *let* yourself dream and *allow* yourself to have.

Start today and do one thing.

Dream bigger. Believe bigger.

You are so much greater than you're letting yourself be.

Dear God,

you know how great I can become. You know what potential and power you've placed inside of me. You know the gifts, talents, and abilities that you've created in me. I thank you so much for showing me and helping me to be everything that you created me to be. I let go of my limited thinking and living any part of my life with limits, doubts, and fears. You are in control of it all. What an awesome feeling it is to know that you, and only you, have my life in your hands and that you're creating me and it to be the amazing masterpiece it will be. I love you, God. Thank you. Yes... Amen.

♥

You give me that stick!"

Let me share a lesson about faith I have so much fun showing Bob.

One of the things Bob and I love to do is get in our car and go for a ride that we call "Go bye-bye."

When we're out driving around and exploring and we see a beautiful lake or pond, we'll stop and get out, and Bob will find just the perfect stick so Bob and I can play "throw the stick in the water and watch me swim and go get it."

Talk about making my tail wiggle non-stop!

And here's how we do it…

Once we find the best stick, Bob will pick it up and walk near the water's edge.

As Bob very slowly brings the stick up in the air and it back behind him like he's getting ready to throw it, I'll get excited!

I'll be on the bank or shore barking and my paws will already be in the water and moving up and down and can't stand still, as my tail wiggles so fast you can't count how quickly it's going round and round.

Just when I think Bob is ready to throw it, Bob will bring his arm back… just a few more inches… and *then*… into the air that stick flies and way, way out into the water it goes.

Without a second of hesitation, I jump in the water and go swimming after it!

I paddle my four paws just as fast as I can, as I wiggle my tail wiggler just like a little propeller, and I do it all at the same time with the biggest happy-boy-dog grunts everyone near the water can hear.

I'm in heaven!

It can be a minute or minutes later, depending on how far Bob throws the stick and how much farther the current may have carried it, when I'll arrive at my stick.

The moment I see it, I grab it in my mouth, lightning fast.

As soon as I grab it, Bob yells, *"Good boy! Cody good boy! Bring it here!"*

With that big stick in my mouth, I turn myself around with such joy and back to Bob I'll swim, just so we can do it over and over again.

As I get closer to the shore and begin walking out of the water and towards Bob, I'll have the biggest smile on my face as Bob says to me, *"You give me that stick!"*

I'll stand there wiggling my tail and grinning as I happily hold that stick in my mouth before releasing it.

Bob and I are in heaven on this earth, having the most fun with each other.

Ah... yet this isn't just another Cody-and-Bob-having-another-great-time-together experience with our throw-the-stick-in-the-water adventure.

This is also God using the unlikeliest of experiences to teach a powerful lesson about what it means to live your faith by faith and belief.

From something as simple as just watching me get excited and love swimming after and grabbing my stick.

We live in a world in which, contained within every experience, is also a wonderful lesson if only you'll look for it.

Think about it...

I wouldn't *desire* to swim after that stick in the water, unless God gave me the desire to do so and that desire was fun, happy and good for me.

I never know how deep or swift the water is I'm swimming in.

I never know what's underneath me as I swim.

I never need to know.

God is underneath me and helping carry me to the desire God has given to me.

I have faith and belief.

A pup's faith and belief that trusts completely and without question.

The kind of faith and belief that's always protecting me, always guiding me, always blessing me, and always assuring me all will always be well.

And it always is and always will be.

It doesn't matter if there are waves and so much distance for me to travel from where I start to swim.

It doesn't matter if I can't see the complete path in front of me to where my stick is.

I go after it and never look back.

For I know, believe, and trust that I *will* arrive to where it is.

And I always do and I always will.

Once I get there—and I always do—that stick is waiting for me to grab, to hold, and to enjoy.

All because God gives me the desire to go after what I want and the faith to believe I will have it.

What if you started living your life doing more of the same?

How *different* could your life be?

How much more fun and fulfilling could it be?

How blessed could you be?

I'll tell you…

"Amazingly blessed!"

The next time you feel God speaking to you with that quiet desire you feel inside, follow God to the shore.

God is about to throw your stick of blessings out in the water in front of you.

It's time for you to go get it.

Dear God,

for so long, I've heard about others doing extraordinary things and living amazing lives because they have faith and belief. I've always thought I could do that too if I ever wanted to. Yet I've not actually done it the way I know I could. In the way you have been calling me to try. On this day, I'm ready to take a bold leap of faith and belief and begin by giving you some of the control of my life. It's tough for me to say "Here's everything in my life God, go ahead and take it all and do with it as you please." You know that for me, that is too much too soon, even though I know deep down that's really what I want to do. So I step out in faith, believing and trusting that you know what's best for me, how it's best for me, where it's best for me, when it's best for me, and with those who are best for me. I ask that you take this small part of my life and show me that I can trust you for a little more of it and then a little more of it. Something inside of me is telling me that we're about to have the best time doing this that I can imagine. It's about to get really fun. I'm ready, dear God. I trust you. I believe in you. I have faith in you. I love you. Thank you. Yes... Amen.

♥

Bark and the door will always be opened"

The desires within you will never end.

Just as soon as you get that desire you've been wanting, you'd better get ready, because right behind it is another one waiting to take its place.

And what a wonderful thing that is.

You're alive and moving forward!

I love teaching Bob a dog's lesson about desire.

Whatever I want I get.

And it all begins by standing at the door.

If I want to go outside and play, all I have to do is look at Bob, or head to the door and wait or bark.

And every time, that door is opened.

It's the same way with your life.

God wants to give you your desires.

All you have to do is knock.

The door you want, or a better one, will always be opened.

You just need to go to the door.

Believe your dream will happen.

Because it will.

Now go to your door of dreams and desires and knock.

My tail is starting to wiggle because I can see it clearly.

And soon...

So will you.

God is already there.

At the door.

Waiting to open it for you.

Dear God,

I am so grateful for the dreams you have placed in my heart. You know the way to them better than anyone. Show me the way to the door that opens to them. Give me the strength and belief to stand patiently and strong until I'm ready and my dreams are ready to become the reality in my life. Thank you. Yes... Amen.

♥

> ## *God will put you in the perfect place you need to be at the perfect time you need to be there"*

It feels good to be in control.

Knowing you are directing your life the way you want it to go feels powerful and invigorating.

So how do you feel when the things you desire seem to take forever to come your way?

Do you easily give up on your desires, or do you hang in there, knowing and believing they are on the way to you?

Bob and I live all over the country, and it's amazing how God puts Bob and me in the perfect places at just the perfect times.

Each place we live gives Bob and me just the things we need to experience, learn, and grow at that time in our lives.

Once we experience all we need and desire to experience, God opens the next door and gives us the new desire for us to go to the next great place.

It never ends.

And it's changed our lives in so many ways for the very best.

God wants to do the same for you.

God has so many perfect places, filled with people that will be just right for you (and you for them), for just the perfect reasons you will be there.

And it is all going to happen in divine, perfect timing.

The important thing is to wait on divine timing to open the doors you'll need that will make it easy and joyful for you to make the changes in your life that you desire to make.

Making them on your own or making them too fast or in the way and timing that isn't best for you won't bring you the best experience you want.

God sees and understands the *big* picture of how every experience and every person and every result will all fit together perfectly.

And at just the right time.

Just hang on a little longer.

Great news and great things are on their way to you.

God is going to make sure you'll be in the perfect place you need to be at the perfect time you need to be there.

Dear God,

so often, okay, maybe always, I want things to happen when I want them to happen and it can be frustrating when they don't. Then I realize I can only do so much on my own. Other people have other things important to them and their lives to live and I can't control what they say or do and when they say or do it. It's time for a fresh new way of living my life. One that puts you in the director's chair for the movie called My Life. You, better than me, or anyone else, know where I am, where I've been, and where I'd like to go. You know what will bring me the greatest happiness, joy, fulfillment, and purpose for my life. And you know the best way to take me to them all. I trust in you. I know that everything you do for me—and I'm so grateful for it all—is for my divine perfect, highest, best, and most happy good. Thank you so much for helping and for always being by my side, dear God. I love you. Thank you. Yes… Amen.

♥

Put yourself into the divine flow and perfect timing for your life"

In your people world, it has been said that timing is everything.

You can have the best plans and ideas, yet if the people who can help you make those dreams a reality are not ready for them, the timing is not right and those plans and ideas may not succeed like you desire.

When your timing *is* just right, then doors of opportunities and oceans of good news can flood your way almost effortlessly.

All because you are in life's perfect flow.

It always amazes Bob at just how perfect my timing is.

For me, it's just the way I'm created, and I'm only being who and what God created me to be.

To Bob, it's as if I always have someone whispering in my ear to think this, do this, go there, and see this, and always at just the best times to do it.

Then it dawned on him…

I *do* have that ear whisperer.

God.

I am always listening to my inner guidance and voice from within, and that voice, God's, is always guiding me to the next best thing to experience, love and enjoy.

Just the way God wants to do for you.

You see, God knows everything you want.

There's nothing you desire that God doesn't already know about and wants you to have *if* it's for your divine perfect and highest, best good.

So, you may be asking, how can you go from where you now are to where you dream and desire to be?

By trusting God to take you there in the divine, perfect way.

Your faith and trust puts you instantly into the flow of life and in synch with divine perfect timing to work in every area of your life.

Once you're in that flow and timing, watch how the right people at just the right times and for the right reasons begin showing up in your life.

And you'll show up in theirs too.

Just the way God is directing it to be.

Give every dream and desire you have to God.

And then trust and listen for the *next* inspired thought and action.

Once you receive it, follow it without hesitation or question.

Get into the divine flow and perfect timing for your life by letting your dreams and desires go to God.

You're going to be amazed at just how beautifully everything you want and everyone you'll need for your greatest joy and happiness will be brought to you.

Dear God,

thank you for showing me just how beautifully choreographed this dance of life truly is. Everything just unfolds so perfectly and wonderfully and without my help. Each day, you show me just how in control you are of this world and my life. Thank you for directing it all so amazingly. I so appreciate every moment of every day. I'm so grateful to have the power of my thoughts and to decide how I want to live my life and whom I want to share it with. You are my best friend, my confidant, my protector, and my provider, and I want it to always be that way. Thank you for teaching me that by my choice, whenever I'm in your divine flow, I'll always be guided and know the perfect way for me to go. You are incredible, God. I love you. Thank you. Yes... Amen.

♥

I'll wait as long as it takes"

You ever watch a dog that loves their owner?

The dog could be at home or in the car, and when the love of their life is away from them, they'll look and keep looking for their best friend and wait patiently for them to return.

No matter how long it takes.

I do it every day.

When Bob leaves our home to do his daily errands and things he likes to do, he'll give me a kiss as he tells me "I'll be home soon," and soon it is, when he always returns.

When we're out in our car going for a ride we call "bye-bye," when Bob gets out of our car to go to the store, fill our car up with gas or go to one of favorite restaurants to get us a treat, I follow him right to the window of our car.

Out that window my head will go and that's where it will stay, looking at Bob and watching where he's going, just waiting for him to walk back to our car.

Whenever he leaves, my tail wiggles, and when he returns, my tail wiggles, and I'll wait wherever we are and for however long it takes because I love him.

As a dog, I have endless patience for the one I love.

Just like God.

And just like God, I'm in no hurry because whatever Bob and I are doing, wherever we're going, we're always going there and doing it *together*.

So many in your people world have such a lack of patience.

Patience for others.

Patience for themselves.

Patience for their dreams.

Patience for God to change their lives and to help them become bigger, better, and more like the person they want to be and take them to everything they can dream of and desire.

They give up too soon.

They think life is passing them by and, along with it, the possibility and potential for change and to experience blessings that can make their lives richer, happier, more loving, and fulfilled.

It's time to be more like us dogs.

It's time to step back from seeing your life so closely and with such judgment.

It's time to be more patient and let life unfold the way it is, and enjoy your life and everything and everyone in it as it does.

Anyone you've ever met and everything that's happened to you are right on schedule and going perfectly according to *the plan*.

And not just your plan.

God's plan for you.

Good things come to those who wait.

Some dreams happen quickly.

The impossible takes just a little longer.

Dear God,

thank you for being so patient, kind, understanding, and loving with me. Thank you for waiting for me to listen to your voice from within and not just listen to it, but have enough faith in myself and in you to follow it. I know now, more than at any time before in my life, you already know what's going to happen in my life for everything, even before anything begins. Today, I know you are so ready to help me, to bless me, and to guide me to every dream in my heart and to all those I've not even let myself go deep inside of me to discover. Take me to it all. I'm ready, dear God. With you, all things are not only possible, they can and will happen in your most divine perfect timing and way that's always for my divine perfect, highest, best and yes, happiest good. I love you, God. Thank you. Yes… Amen.

♥

> *I love you for who you are. Now let me show you who you can be."*

Life has a way of bringing you the unlikeliest of people to be your teachers.

Animals too.

Bob's is named Cody.

That's me!

Bob loves knowing I'm one of the greatest teachers and inspiring living creatures God could've ever put into his life.

And if you've ever had a dog, loved a dog, or spent time with a dog, you'll know it's the same for you too.

I give Bob unconditional and unlimited love every second of every day.

In my eyes, Bob is the love of my life, my best friend and companion, and I love treating him like royalty all the time.

I see Bob and accept him the way God loves and sees me.

I'm Bob's dog, Cody.

A living, breathing God-created animal with four legs, green eyes, floppy ears, and little tail, inspiring Bob each day to go higher, do more, and become greater.

When was the last time someone did that for you?

Who is inspiring you *right now*?

Who is speaking faith, hope, belief, and greatness into your life?

Who is inspiring you to become bigger, better, and more than you are and have ever been?

God has the right people you're seeking and those who are seeking you, waiting for you right now.

You just need to let them in.

You may be asking, *"How do I find them and let them into my life?"*

Ask God to bring them to you and you to them in life's divine perfect way and timing.

Whatever and whoever you are searching for is searching for you right now.

The key is to trust divine timing and the divine way for it to all happen just the way it should.

When you do, then get ready.

In the coming days, you'll be shown that your prayers have been heard.

You'll meet people who'll give you the missing piece to an answer and a direction you've been searching for.

You'll meet people who'll say the perfect word or tell you things you need to hear that will in some way inspire you and you inspire them.

You'll meet people and be at the right place at just the right time that'll give you and them just what you need that'll help take each of you to the next perfect step in your life's journey.

You'll be shown that in this life there is no chance, randomness, or coincidence.

You'll be shown time and time again, because you are trusting God for *all* the things in your life, that God is taking care of *everything* in your life.

You are loved for who you are.

God is now going to show you just who you can be.

Dear God,

it amazes me to think how great I can be. There are no limits to what I can have, be, do, or experience. With faith and belief, all things are possible. I'm so grateful and so appreciate your reminding me that I'm your child. I come from you. You are inside of me. You are me and you are for me. And if you are for me, then nothing and no one can be against me. Ever. Thank you, God, for bringing into my life just the best people I so desire who can be good for me and me good for them. I love helping people. I love inspiring people and knowing I'm making a positive difference in their lives. Help me and inspire me to do more, to be greater, and to live an unlimited life of abundance, joy, happiness, love, peace, and fulfillment. It's all because of you, dear God. I love you. Thank you. Yes… Amen.

♥

7

LISTENING
TO THE VOICE
WITHIN

> *How can you hear the call from within, if so much of your day is spent thinking about the things from without?"*

Inside of every dog and person on this earth is a call and a nudge that keeps reminding us in subtle ways of the things we want.

I listen to this call every day as I think of the things I enjoy and want to do, like rolling on my back in the grass, and I keep my thinking focused on doing that *until* I experience it.

And I *always* do.

I never think about those things outside of me (the things from "without") of what someone said, what someone posted or texted, or how I think someone looks at me, as triggers for my being upset and resentful and staying that way for hours, days, or months.

I like staying in the God Zone.

The place inside of my body where I'm perfectly connected and listening and communicating with God, who created me.

Right now at this moment, God is communicating with you.

It's the divine call from within, and it's always flowing to you throughout the day and night.

Let yourself hear its call.

Dear God,

thank you for being so good to me. Thank you for reminding me throughout the day that you are my best friend who is always with me, talking to me in ways I can know and understand, guiding me, protecting me, blessing me, and helping me. You know me better than I know myself, and I want to trust you more and more for everything in my life. Thank you for showing me how to do that. Thank you. Yes... Amen.

♥

We're always connected"

Once you've experienced it, you can never go back.

It's that *feeling*.

That feeling and connection you get when you're looking at us.

Spend time with one of us dogs and you will sense a purity and connection that we have to the Divine, right there in that moment.

A connection you cannot get from anyone or anywhere else.

As you look and interact with us, it feels like we have the phone line, the always-on communication line, right to God, as if we've crossed over to the other side and are living in your world and the God spirit world, both at the same time.

We are.

You know *why* you feel that way?

You came from there too.

As much as you can love this life and all those and everything in it, you want to know that the God spirit world that you and all of us came from and will return to is still there right now, and available to you.

And every day you are with us, we keep showing you, "Yes, it is."

And so are those that are in it, who are right now available to you.

To guide you.

To help you.

To protect you.

To bless you.

To show you the way, as they speak to us and we speak to you, through a thought, a feeling, an inspiration, an idea, and they speak to you with the silent voice you feel deep inside that only you can hear and only you can know.

Open your heart, soul, and mind and let yourself be touched by us, and by the unseen and *always felt* power of God, to do phenomenal things in your life.

And don't worry about how and when and where you'll find that connection and power.

We're here to help you.

Just keep looking at us, and we'll take you right to it every time.

Dear God,

I know I live in a bigger world than the one I can see and experience in the here and now. A bigger world where the stars and the universe surround me, and one that you control with absolute perfection. I'm part of that world, for I come from you. I'm your child and your creation, and so are everyone and every animal that has lived and will ever live. I've always wondered what happens to us when we leave these earthly bodies after this life's journey has been completed. I now know my life and who I am will never end. You are eternal, God, and I'm your child that you've created to be eternal just like you. We are one and will always be. The people and animals I love will always be those I love, and they will always love me, because our lives together will never end. We are all eternal and everlasting creations of love and of yours. Thank you for my angels who are always with me, blessing me, guiding me, and helping me. I love you, angels. I love you, God. I love knowing that we are right now and will always be together and forever in each other's lives. I love you, God. I love you, life. Thank you. Yes... Amen.

♥

The road you travel is only revealed step by step as you travel it"

You know what I love?

The unknown, and I never have any fear of it.

I know that the only way to get to where you want to go is to move forward along a path that is only revealed as you travel it.

Bob and I meet many people who have dreams, desires, and longings they'd love to experience but never will because they're afraid of the unknown.

They want to see every road they'll travel.

They want to know every step they'll take.

They want a preview of what's going to happen along the way.

And they want to know all of these things *before* they will take a first step on the way.

God doesn't do things like that.

That's where faith comes in.

The bigger your faith, the bigger and greater your life will be.

God wants us to trust and give God the permission to direct every step in our lives.

You give that permission by doing two simple things:

Ask for divine guidance and let go of the need to know the way *before* you start.

Have faith that God will be there in front of you, guiding you *every* step of the way.

God will.

Each and every day, I live my life by faith, a pup's faith, that never fails me or lets me down.

The God that directs, protects, and inspires Bob and me is the same God that will do those things for you.

Dear God,

thank you for helping me to let go of any fear that has kept me from living the life you created me to live. Thank you for showing me that as your divine creation, I have no limits in the life I can live and love except for those I place upon myself by my belief in them. You created me and know everything that brings me happiness. I let go of all limitations and thank you for inspiring me to trust and follow your direction for my life, even when I may not know what the next step may be. You do. I put all my faith and trust in you for my life. I know you are putting everyone and everything in my life in divine perfect order and timing. I love you. Thank you. Yes... Amen.

♥

Listen to your angels whispering to you"

You have good company.

Those you've known who've left their bodies from this earth and are now back to spirit are surrounding you this moment.

Even those you've never met, like a grandparent, great grandparent or friend from your family you may have never known, are surrounding you and care about everything about you.

They are with you right now.

Yes, you may not see them, but their power to help, guide, and change your life is always there, always on, and always ready to help you simply by your acknowledging them and asking them to help you.

And they joyfully will.

I listen to my angels.

I intuitively and instinctively know they are always with me and will always be.

Bob loves watching me connect with those angels.

I can be so busy and right in the middle of doing something that I'll just stop to *turn my head to hear and to sense something.*

Yes, we dogs can hear things you humans cannot.

Bob knows me so well and watches me so many times that he knows the difference between a noise I hear on the outside and *a noise I hear from the inside.*

Inside of my soul.

It's that *certain way* I stop and pause whatever I'm doing to receive that moment's message and inspiration.

The message from my angels whispering to me.

Those moments of inspiration and guidance for me have never stopped.

Nor will they.

My communication line is always clear and always open.

What about yours?

When's the last time you listened to the voice from within?

God moves in mysterious ways, and if you think that what you see around you is all there is that surrounds you, *it isn't.*

It's time for you to listen to your angels whispering to you.

They know things you don't.

They want to help guide you to things that will bring you joy and happiness.

They are protecting you every moment of every day.

And they can guide you to the life you desire, every God-directed step of the way.

Dear God,

thank you for all of my angels. So many times in my life, I've felt the hands of a power I never could understand, yet I just knew it was something beyond my control and something unexplainable and unseen. Now I know. It's you and your angels. My angels, who are always with me, guiding me, helping me, blessing me, protecting me, and inspiring me. I'm so grateful to you and to them for it all. Show me to how connect with my angels so that I may do so every day in every way. I love you and all of my friends, family, loved ones, animals, and those I may never have known, yet who know me, that have departed in the physical form from this earth but who are with me right here and right now and will always be. I love you, God. I love you, my angels. Thank you. Yes... Amen.

♥

Which way are you pointing me to, God?"

Have you ever thought about what God has planned for your life?

Have you ever wondered what might happen, how it will happen, and when?

If you answered *"Yes,"* you're in good company.

Whether those in your people world admit or not, most, if not all, of you have asked yourselves these questions.

Bob loves watching me receive the answers.

Like when I go outside to play.

So many times, just as soon as my feet touch the deck, patio or grass, I'll just stop and look around.

It's as if God is sitting down next to me, with a hand on my face and body as we are both looking out at what's in front of us, and saying to me, *"Cody, what do you want to do today?"*

I'll just smile as I soak in the warmth of the sun, the freshness of the air I'm breathing, the gift and miracle of this new day, and all the sights I'm seeing, hearing, and smelling.

As Bob watches me, it's as if I'm answering, *"I'm so happy being in this moment. What do you, God, want us to do?"*

And with a nudge inside I feel to move my feet and body forward, it's as if God answers, *"Let's go over there,"* and off we go to discover the first gifts this day is about to bring.

Imagine living more of your life in the same way.

Imagine living your life where more of your day is *guided by the inspiration from the divine voice within,* who is taking you to the next great thing and experience you desire and need for you to grow bigger and better.

God has every day and night full of *"Let's go over there"* experiences waiting for you.

And the eight magic words that will take you to them are *"Which way are you pointing me to, God?"*

Dear God,

I am so thankful that you are always with me every moment of every day. You are the best friend I could ever ask for. I want to trust my life to your guidance and direction. You, better than anyone else, know what brings me the greatest joy and happiness. You, better than anyone else, know how and why you created me and have given to me the gifts, talents, and abilities you've blessed me with. Thank you for helping me to use them to the fullest of my God-given abilities so that I may touch the lives of your other children and animals in the biggest and best ways. I am so happy and blessed. My life is amazing, and it's all because of you. Thank you. Yes… Amen.

♥

Let God be good to you"

Let's pretend for a moment.

You have someone who thinks the world of you.

This person is very successful in life and loves to share their blessings with anyone they can.

This person also has "connections," *big* connections, with the people who can make *big* things happen in significant ways.

For years, this person has wanted to help you but could not, because you either let it be known to everyone that you think you know it all, think you need to do it all, or think you need to control it all.

How would you feel, knowing that?

You could say we dogs have someone like that in our lives.

God.

The difference between us and you in our story is that *we let God direct us and bless us every moment of every day.*

It has been said that God helps those who help themselves.

And how do you help yourself?

By being a receptive open channel that *lets you be guided and blessed in all the ways your creator knows are best for you.*

Your life can be so amazing and so much more and better than what you're living at this moment.

You haven't even begun to scratch the surface of the kind of fantastic life that is waiting for you to live, love, and enjoy.

Get ready to be blessed in ways that are about to amaze you.

Dear God,

I am so grateful for the dreams and desires inside of me. You know exactly what I want and what I need, and the best way for only those things that are divinely right for me to put into my life. I give you my life and everything in it, and I thank you for blessing it and guiding it so perfectly in every way. I love you. Thank you. Yes... Amen.

♥

> ## *Ask God this: 'How can I let into my life, what you want to put into it?'"*

You all want so many things.

It seems you have more desires than you have time and money to fulfill them.

Yet you never stop desiring more.

So stop for moment.

Have you ever wondered what God *wants* to give you?

Have you ever wondered how God wants to give it to you?

Have you ever wondered when God wants to give it to you?

So few of you in your people world ever stop to ask yourself such questions.

You're so busy living in your tiny world that you don't have the time to let God lead you to the bigger world.

You think *you* know best how to bring all of what you want into your life.

So how has all of that been working out so far?

As Bob watches me each and every day, he marvels at how I'm an open channel to anything and everything God wants to bring to me to experience.

Like you, my desires for more never stop.

And that's a wonderful thing!

Unlike most of you, I *let* myself go to whatever desire is calling my name, *wherever* and *whenever* it's calling my name.

Without saying a word, I'm constantly talking to and asking God, *"Show me how I can let into my life everything you want to put into it."*

And God hears me and always answers with *"How about this, Cody? How about this? How about this?"*

Imagine if you let yourself connect with God the way I do.

Imagine how different your life would be.

Imagine *what* you *could* become.

The possibilities would be limitless, and so would the life you'd *now* be living.

A life without limits.

That sounds incredible, doesn't it?

Other people have lived it.

Other people are living it.

And so can you.

Today, do something that you haven't done in a while or maybe even ever.

Talk to God.

This time, ask God a new question.

"How can I let into my life, what you want to put into it?"

The answer is about to change your life.

Dear God,

I'm so ready to let myself start thinking, believing, and expecting a bigger, better life. A life I can live, love, enjoy, and inspire others to. A life where miracle upon miracle of never-ending, never-stopping blessings pour forth from you and rain down and flood my life. A life where I'm using every gift, talent, and ability that you've so lovingly blessed me with to the fullest of my God-given abilities so I can be a blessing to others. I know deep down inside of me that your plans for my life are amazing and are so far above and beyond anything I can know or imagine. From this day on, I let go of any fears, doubts, and worries. By my faith and belief in you, in me, and in us, I release the unlimited power you've placed inside of me to become all that I can be and to live and love the extraordinary life you are calling and taking me to, this day and all the days to come. I love you, God. Thank you. Yes... Amen.

♥

8

FOLLOWING
THE INSPIRATION
WITHIN

When it comes to inspiration... sighs matters"

It can be a wonderful thing, to have clear and concise directions and instructions for the things you want to do.

It just feels better knowing you're on the right path, doing things the right way, because others went before you to help show you just what to do and how to do it.

How quickly you realize that the need for knowing can keep you from growing.

It can keep you from traveling down your own trail and towards a destiny that's only *your* own and one that God has designed so perfectly for each of us.

I always trust my guidance from within in everything I live, do, and experience.

Watching me live my amazing blessed life has taught Bob a powerful lesson...

"How are you going to know if you never find out?"

God's guidance from the *inside* will always keep you right on perfect track on the *outside*.

You'll know what to *say*.

You'll know what to *do*.

You'll know where to *go*.

You'll know *whom* to meet and *when*.

And you'll know when to *stay* and when to *go*.

God's guidance from within will never fail you.

Ever.

It's when you start listening more to the world and others that you take detours and side roads you never need to take.

You live in a world where the more outrageous something is, the more outrageous someone does, and the more outrageous someone says, that's the accepted and embraced way to live.

Ah… living from the world's opinion and not from your divinely inspired own can really do a number on you if you let it.

The world will try to scare you, every chance you give it.

Those things you love to do and always did are now wrong.

And when it comes to anything called God, that divine guidance and small voice that speaks to you from within is no longer to be trusted.

Are you ready to let go of the world's craziness?

Good, because I have a message for you…

It's time to get "unfreaked out" about your life.

The things you used to do are still the things you can do if you'll let go of the newfound fears, worries, doubts, and anxieties you've now attached to them.

Let yourself get back to the free-flowing, good-feeling thoughts you had about the things you loved doing in the past.

You can still enjoy them now… today… this moment.

Get back to your God-given, inspired, and directed perfect guidance from within.

Stay true to your dreams, wherever they may lead you.

When it comes to inspiration, sighs *matters.*

That inspiration will always take you to the perfect places, at the perfect times, with the perfect people, and just the way God is directing it to be.

Dear God,

you more than anyone know what I want and why I want it. I ask that you fill my life with your desires and inspirations because as my creator, you know exactly the things, experiences, and moments that will bring me the greatest joy, fulfillment, and happiness. Thank you for raining down blessing after never-ending blessing in every part of my life. Let me uplift and be an inspiration to all those I meet. You are such an inspiration to me, dear God, and I love you. Thank you. Yes... Amen.

♥

> *Ask yourself where you want to go to be the most inspired, and then go there and find out"*

Bob loves watching me receive inspiration.

One of our favorite things to do is go for our daily car rides we call "Go bye-bye."

Each time we go out, we try to find a place we've never been to.

Once we get there, without hesitation, I know *exactly* where to go to begin that day's brand new adventure.

Of all the places I can choose to put my head to the ground, sniff, and run to, I always choose the *best* place, the most *fun* place, the most *satisfying* place, the most *inspiring* place, because God is guiding me to it.

I don't have Siri, Google Maps, or any social media app on my dog phone telling me where to go or where my friends are.

I have the greatest GPS of all.

God.

The one who always guides me to inspiration after endless inspiration.

Like me, you are hardwired with an always-on and always-by-your-side-and-inside-you source of perfect guidance every moment of every day when you take God with you everywhere you go.

So smile and relax.

God knows where *your* next inspiration will be found.

It's time for you to let God take you to it.

So go ahead.

Slide on over to the passenger side.

Let God be the driver of your life and take you to it.

You are in for an amazing ride.

Dear God,

thank you for taking the wheel for the journey called my life. You know just the right ways to go, the perfect timing and ways for us to get there, the right people to meet and places for us to see, and the most fulfilling experiences all along the way. I so appreciate knowing and trusting that my life and everything and everyone in it, is in the best hands with you. You are extraordinary. I am extraordinary. I love you. Thank you. Yes... Amen.

♥

This is a great place that's on my way to the next great place"

So many of those in your people world think they're stuck right where they are.

The only thing that keeps anyone stuck is their *belief* that they're stuck.

Good thing dogs never believe it.

In all the years Bob and I have been best friends sharing and loving life together, we have been so blessed to live all over the United States and to travel through most of those states.

Every place we move to and each home we live in feels like we own it and it's just like "our" home.

And talk about exciting!

Months before our next big moving adventure, Bob will talk to me and ask me throughout the day and night…

"Cody, where would you like to go?"

"Cody, where do you think we should live?"

"Cody, where would you like to move?"

And even though Bob is speaking in English, I *know* what Bob is saying.

As the days pass and Bob talks to me about our move, Bob can tell what place gets me *most* excited just by my response to it when Bob mentions its name.

When the time comes that *"we"* decide where our next adventure will be, Bob starts getting our boxes packed, we go to local charities to drop off things we no longer need, and we are both getting so excited about the big day that's fast approaching.

Words cannot express how exhilarating going someplace new is.

Talk about making my little tail wiggle!

For Bob and me, each new place is like a giant blank chalkboard.

From the first day we get there to one year later, we think, "*What will we be writing on that chalkboard?*"

What new *people* will we meet?

What new *things* will we do?

What new *places* will we visit?

What new *experiences* will we have?

Each new place we've lived has, and still does have, our own unique chalkboard that we've created, shared, lived, and loved *together*.

Like us, God wants you to have a life of big giant chalkboards of new places filled with new people, new experiences, and new blessings.

They are all out there waiting for you right now.

All that's needed for you to experience them is to let go of the routine, the predictable, and the comfortable and let yourself *go to what's calling your name.*

Let yourself follow your divine inspiration.

When you have God as your life partner and friend, you are never stuck where you are.

It's time for you to get excited about your life again.

The place you're now living is only a great place that's on your way to the next great place God wants to take you to.

Dear God,

you have so many great things waiting for me to experience, and on this day I ask you to take me to them. I let go of the attachments I've placed on anything and anyone in my life out of fear. You created me to do more, be more, and have more, and I thank you for every divine desire you have placed inside of me. I'm ready to go anywhere and do anything you want me to. My life is yours, and so is everything in it. Thank you. Yes... Amen.

♥

Every moment in every day, born again in every way"

Imagine having a fresh start and new beginning every second you're alive.

How do you think that would feel?

Do you think it's even possible?

Possible?

Not only *is* it possible, but if you're not giving yourself those brand new moments each and every moment, you're keeping yourself from a life of blessings.

I love showing Bob how it's done.

The first thing to do is to start living your life less from the opinions of experts and others, and more from your God-given intuition and wisdom.

Dogs don't do focus groups or social media testing.

Dogs couldn't care less about numbers and statistics and sharings with friends, friending, or liking me or us.

Dogs will never talk about the past, problems, or what was.

We bark, wiggle, and giggle at what is and what soon will be.

We act from divine guidance and connection that doesn't need a screen to look at every few minutes we're not busy doing something else or a web to be connected to at the beginning of each day for assurance, communication, or guidance.

A dog is God's eyes, ears, nose, and paws that act from instinct and guidance that comes only when one is connected to the Divine.

And you can be too.

I live *inside* the new moment of every new day, and that moment is like a brand new world to me.

To me, it's as if…

Every moment in every day, I'm born again in every way.

It never stops.

It's time for you to experience that too.

Let yourself be happy and watch how much happier your outer world becomes.

Dear God,

I'm so grateful with the blessing and gift of my life, with each new day and with each new moment. A happy life is made up of happy moments, and I ask that you show me to how fill my life with more and more of those happy moments each and every day. For this is the day that you have made, and I want it and will rejoice and be happy in it. Help me to listen to your divine inspiration and guidance. Give me the belief and trust to follow it. I know it is and will always be perfect and just exactly what I want and need at just the perfect time I want and need it. Thank you. Yes… Amen.

♥

Where you are is not where you're going to be"

Think back to a year ago and look at how much your life has changed.

Think back to four years ago and look at all the changes that have happened.

Incredible, isn't it?

Just as planned.

On God's plan.

If there's anything in your life right now that isn't bringing you happiness, and joy, just stayed tuned...

Where you are is not where you're going to be.

One of the most fun things I love to show Bob is how *connected* I am to God by living my life in *the now* and *the next*.

To me, the past is like a mist in the air that quickly evaporates once I experience living it.

And I never look back at what was and wonder where it went.

I know that things are *never* the same going back a second time around.

While places and things can slowly change, God created all of us to *quickly* change, many times, in the blink of an eye and without our truly realizing just how much.

I know instinctively from God that where I am is not where I'm going to be, either on this day or in the tomorrows that will follow.

And it will be the same for you.

God is going to take you places that are going to *astonish* you.

Take you places that will *fulfill* you.

Take you places that will *inspire* you.

Take you places that will reveal new wonders and mysteries you never would've considered today, yesterday, and even three years ago.

Take you places different from where you are.

So smile.

You have so much to look forward to.

Where you are is not where you're going to be, and you're soon about to live it, love it, and discover why.

Dear God,

I'm so grateful and thankful for this life you have blessed me with. I'm so thankful for all the things that I've lived so far. Everything and everyone has been a blessing and a teacher on this amazing journey called my life. I'm so excited for all the new that is waiting for me to discover, to live, to love, and to enjoy. I trust you completely to take me to every good thing you have planned for me, and I thank you with all my heart. I love you. Thank you. Yes... Amen.

♥

All things work together for everyone's good, at just the right time, and not a moment sooner or later"

Time.

Those in your people world live by it.

They get stressed about it.

They wish they had more of it.

Have you ever wondered why some things happen in life at the most unexpected times?

When you get into the flow of divine perfect timing, the answer becomes clear...

All things work together for everyone's good, at just the right time, and not a moment sooner or later.

Like all dogs, I'm so in synch with the flow of God's perfect divine timing that it's a marvel for Bob to watch.

I always love to go outside, but I won't want to do it until I know the timing is just right.

Take playing with God's wild creatures.

I know that if I go outside too soon, I either won't find any animals or, if I do, they may not be ready to play and could be scared off too easily and quickly.

So I wait.

I have faith.

I believe that good things are *just* about to happen...

If only I'm just a little more patient, God will instinctively inspire me to know "Now is the perfect time, Cody."

And it always is!

The trees I always visit with only twigs, branches, and leaves are now filled with squirrels I chase up and down and all around.

And all of us, the squirrels and me, loving it and just having the times of our lives!

All because I waited, listened, and then acted from *inspiration*.

So what if you could trust a little more?

What if you could be a little more patient for the things you want?

What if you truly *"let go and let God"* and handed everything in your life over to the power that created and sustains you?

What if you waited, listened, and then acted from inspiration?

How different do you think your life could be?

Once you understand God's hand in everything, you'll trust God's hand to guide to you in anything.

Everything you *dream* of.

Everything you *desire*.

Everything you *believe* in.

Everything you'll let yourself have because you'll feel *worthy* to receive it.

It's time for you to smile again.

God has you and all of us covered, big time.

Those things you want, or something better, will happen.

Whether it's your life or that of any other God-created divine person and creature that lives on this amazing earth, *all things work together for everyone's good, at just the right time, and not a moment sooner or later.*

All in God's perfect timing.

Dear God,

I so appreciate you and the perfect timing for everything in my life. I know at times I can be so impatient because I want things to happen the way I want them to happen and when I want them to happen. Yet, I know deep down, that's not the way life works. It's all in your divine perfect timing for my and everyone else's divine perfect, highest, best good. I trust you for everything in my life. I am so grateful for this day, my life, and all the people and blessings I have in it. I am so happy and excited all the wonderful blessings and experiences you have planned and are taking me to right now. Thank you. Yes... Amen.

♥

> ## When taking action comes from inspiration, it's exhilarating and powerful. When action comes from motivation or guilt, it's rarely satisfying."

Ever notice the difference in how you feel, when you do the things you *want to do* rather than doing the things you think you *should* do?

Big difference.

That's because when taking action comes from inspiration, it's exhilarating and powerful.

When action comes from motivation or guilt, it's rarely satisfying.

There's a good reason for that.

We are created to create and to live our lives from inspiration.

Divine inspiration.

When we live a more inspired life, a more joyful and fulfilling life is always the result.

I know.

Boy, do I know it.

I *never* do anything unless it's something *I want to do.*

Something I'm inspired to do.

And there's never a moment or a day that I'm not the happiest boy dog God created me to be.

So few of you can say the same.

Not that you can't.

It's just that you won't.

You're just so tough on yourself.

You live by the belief that says, *"The harder, tougher, more denying and unenjoyable something is, the better it's got to be for you."*

Where does that come from?

You're always so busy being busy doing the things that you *almost* want to do, that you rarely let yourself do the things you *really* want to do.

It's time to let go of living your life by any beliefs keeping you from enjoying the divine-inspired life God has created and wants to give you.

Starting today, look at the things you're doing and believing.

For each of them, ask yourself a simple question: Does this *inspire* me?

If not, let God show you how to change them.

God will.

You'll sense something *changing.*

You'll start to feel *different.*

You'll start feeling happier.

That's God, letting you know God hears you and is helping you.

Get ready.

Your life is about to transform before your eyes.

Dear God,

thank you for showing me how to live the inspired life. You created me to have the dreams and desires of my heart, and I'm so grateful that you're showing me how to do so. I sense that my life is changing for the best and the happiest. I let everything you desire to put into my life, come into my life. I can do all things through you. Thank you. I love you. Yes... Amen.

♥

When are you going to let me take you to it?"

I always know where the good stuff is.

If it's hidden, I'll find it and I'll get to it before anyone else.

And I love taking Bob with me to see it so I can enjoy it with him.

God didn't create this amazing life, this amazing world, and all the good things and experiences that are found in it, just for God alone.

It's created for us.

And God wants to share all of it with you, if only you'll let yourself enjoy it.

"Oh," you might be thinking, *"it's just not that easy."*

We dogs know.

You like control.

So we have a question: How have all those years and time you've spent trying to control everything in your life been working out for you?

Right now, you have someone who wants to be a partner in your life.

Yet that someone will only come into your life by your invitation.

We know you know who it is.

I want you to try something.

Go ahead and pick anything you'd like to achieve, experience, or have.

Make it big enough so that you'll know, when it happens and how it happens, you can see God's help in all of it.

Make it small enough so that your entire world of happiness doesn't depend on it.

And then put it out there.

Begin to trust and believe God is on it and is going to take you to it.

Simply hold on to that thought and don't let it go.

Then watch how things begin *changing* and *moving* in your life.

Moving in your life that lets you know that not only does God *hear* you, God is *helping* you.

Then get ready.

The right people will begin showing up.

The things you need to see, hear, and know will begin being revealed to you in such ways that all of it could never be just a coincidence.

Inspirations and ideas will begin to be received by you.

The perfect plan of action and timing to take action will be known to you.

Your life will begin to be transformed.

You see, for years God has been asking you, *"When are you going to let me take you to it?"*

This is the day you'll answer, *"How about today?"*

Dear God,

every day and every moment is brand new, and I let go of the old that has helped me get to the bold. I'm at a new place in my life today. I'm a new person and being made fresh and new every minute of every single day. Thank you, God. You are so amazing and wonderful. I open my hands and place them in yours as I hold tightly to you in love, faith, belief, and trust. The rest of my life is going to be the best of my life. I know I have all the time, talent, and ability I'll ever need to do your will and live the life of my dreams. And I know—yes, I truly know deep down inside of me—that you are taking me everywhere you desire and have planned for me to experience and to be. My love for you knows no limits, God. Thank you. Yes... Amen.

♥

9

GOING FROM
WHERE YOU ARE TO
ANYWHERE YOU
WANT TO BE

> ## *You have the desire because God has the desire to give it to you*"

Desire is an elusive thing.

You try to look for and find it, and you don't.

Yet it finds you when you least expect it.

So what are the things you desire?

More money?

More opportunity?

More friends?

More love?

More fun, happiness, and joy?

If you have a desire for the good and positive things in this life, you can be sure that those desires are coming direct to you from God.

Bob loves watching me, and how I live my desires every moment of every day.

Like you, I was born with desires.

Unlike so many of those in your people world, I never stop having those desires and seeing them become realities every day of my life.

The more desires I have and let myself be led to, the happier I get.

And the happier I am, the more things I desire.

And the more things I desire, the more things I get to enjoy!

Talk about having an amazing great and blessed life!

How about you?

Is your life so blessed that you have no more room for more blessings and joy to come into it?

Have you let yourself desire the good things, the *big* things, the crazy *huge* things that make you smile every time you look at or think about them?

God created you so that God can live through you, as you, right now.

Think about that.

God is being you *right now.*

And if God created it all and keeps creating it all, don't you think God wants to experience and enjoy it all?

And do it with and through you!

It's time for you to start thinking differently.

See yourself as God sees you.

As a priceless and precious creation that knows no limits or boundaries in experiences.

Those desires you feel are inside of you right now for a good reason…

You have the desire because God has the desire to give it to you.

Dear God,

I thank you for this new day and all the seconds, minutes, and hours in it I will have—to dream big, believe big, expect big, and receive big all the things I so desire. I get the feeling, deep down inside of me, that you can give me anything in this life, if I only I would ask and believe I can have it. I am your child, and I'm worthy of every good and perfect gift that comes from you, dear God. I love knowing that! And even more, I love believing and expecting that! Starting right now, I take the limits off of you and ask that you bring me every joyful and happy desire I have. Take me to every thing and experience you desire for us to have. For your desires are my desires, and my desires are your desires. We are made for each other. We are one for each other. We will always and forever be as one with each other. I love you with everything inside of me, dear God. Thank you. Yes… Amen.

♥

> # *If you keep telling the same life story, you'll keep getting the same life experiences"*

How do you think it would feel if you never had to tell your life story to anyone anymore?

What if the only story you'd tell is the one that describes what you *want* to happen and not a word about whatever *did* happen?

How do you think that would feel?

You're probably thinking, *"Now, that would be amazing!"*

I've got good news for you…

That can be your story if you'll give yourself permission to start telling it.

One of the things Bob just loves about me is that I never tell a story about anything to anyone.

I just live and love each moment of my life and do so with joy and happiness.

And I'm never disappointed.

God has made things *so* easy for you.

Your belief determines the direction and experiences of your life.

And if you're still living in the past with the hurts, angers, remorse and "what could have beens," then that's what you're going to keep creating more of, in your life.

Start telling a new story.

And not the way it is. The way you desire it to be.

And then watch what happens.

Dear God,

you sure know how to get my attention. After years of telling the same old story about my relationships, friends, family, jobs, and experiences, so much of it just makes me unhappy every time I tell it. The message I'm getting from you is, I don't have to tell it or anything to anyone anymore, not even to myself. That I can tell a brand new story, a happier story and inspiring and uplifting story of the life I'm now living and will be living. Thank you for teaching me that, in my life, what I think about I bring about. With your help, I want to. I will keep my thoughts and words on the things I want, it will bring me happiness when I think about them, and I'm going to let go of the rest. Everything and everyone in my past have all helped me to get to the place I now am, and I'm grateful for them. I bless them and let them go with love and blessings. Today is a new day, one filled with incredible joy and unlimited possibilities for me to be, do, or have anything I can dream and desire. That's the life I choose. That's the life I will live. Thank you, dear God for leading, guiding, and inspiring me to it. I love you. Thank you. Yes... Amen.

♥

This just in... There's no age limit or expiration date for dreams"

Those in your people world make us dogs shake our heads.

We see so many of you treat your dreams like old food.

You quickly throw them away once you've convinced yourself they're past their expiration date.

We dogs have some news for you…

Your dreams have no expiration date.

I have lots of dreams.

Yes, dogs *do* have dreams.

My dreams are in the form of desires, and each day I turn one desire after another into my reality.

I don't have a calendar.

I don't have a yearly planner.

I *instinctively* know that God is ready to give me my dreams and desires or something better.

God moves as soon as we move, and we move by opening our thinking to have faith and trust for those things we desire to have happen in our life.

You might think it's too late, you're too old, or you're too anything else for your dreams come true.

And you'd be wrong.

God knows whom you need to know.

God knows where you need to go.

God knows how you need to grow.

And God can take you to all of it just as soon as you're ready.

How about letting today be that day?

Dear God,

thank you for inspiring me with the hope that I can have the dreams I desire, no matter what excuses I've held onto that have kept me from having and living those dreams. I let go of living my life not being authentic to myself, and to the things I know deep down I want and will bring me the happiness I seek. You know where I am, and you know the perfect way to get me to where you desire me to be. I put my trust in you and so appreciate every blessing that was, is, and will be to come. Thank you. Yes... Amen.

♥

Life will give you whatever you ask"

The things you want.

They just never end.

Just the way it's supposed to be.

Your dreams and desires never stop, and once a dream becomes reality, a new dream comes along to take its place.

Those desires of yours can be described as just another way of your "asking" for the things you want to have, experience, and enjoy.

And God and this life will give them to you.

The question is, *"Are you asking big enough?"*

Bob will tell you that if there were a college course on the topic of asking, I would ace it.

My asking and desiring are one and the same.

Every day, I desire new and wonderful experiences, and those desires become my asking to God for them to happen.

And God answers each and every time...

"Here it is Cody, it's yours. Enjoy it!"

If asking is so powerful, *so* powerful in fact, that *"Ask and you shall receive"* has been immortalized as words untold numbers of people have lived by for thousands of years, then why won't you let yourself ask for the things you *really* want and not just the things you *believe* you can have?

God truly will give you the desires of your heart.

If only you'll ask.

Bob likes to tell people a story that brings this point home, literally and figuratively.

For years, Bob's sister dreamed of having a little farm with some acreage and a cozy home that she and her husband could love.

They had a nice home they had lived in for more than 40 years, and in the back of their minds, a part of them believed it was too late to have their dream.

Yet the bigger part of Bob's sister's belief kept telling her that *it's never too late to have your dream.*

The message she felt from God was *"Don't you dare let it go."*

So she quietly talked to God and asked for her dream.

Whenever Bob and his sister would talk about her dream, she would always say, "Maybe some day, someone will knock on our door and want to buy our house, and then we can buy our dream home in the country."

Most people would simply laugh upon hearing such fanciful talk about dreams.

As if one day, someone with money would magically appear at their door with an offer to buy that door and the whole house that went along with it.

One day, that someone knocked at their door.

She answered it.

It was the person standing in front of her whom God sent to answer Bob's sister's prayers and to buy her home.

She asked. God answered.

They got their farm.

All in perfect timing.

God has a world of people who are ready to stand at your door and answer your dreams.

It's time you start asking for your dreams. It's time for you to call them in.

God already knows the way to your house and your heart.

Dear God,

I can never know how and why so many amazing things in this life happen, yet I know they do. As I look back on my life, there have been many times when the things I hoped for, and even better ones, have happened unexpectedly and it just surprised me. Things I could have never made happen on my own. Things I had no idea were about to happen. Yet you knew. You were the one who made them happen. I've lived my life long enough now to realize there isn't anything called "coincidence" or "chance." Everything in this life and this world happens in divine perfect order, and you are the one orchestrating it all. And you know what's even more amazing? I'm your child. I'm the one you created, and we are forever connected as one. My asking to you is very simple: Guide my life, every part of it, and make it everything you know it can be. It's yours. I'm yours. I am so blessed in every way, and I always will be, every day. And it's all because of you, dear God. I love you. Thank you. Yes... Amen.

♥

God never gives you a dream because it fits your budget"

What would you do if you didn't have to go to a "job" every day?

How big would you dream if you had a bank full of money and could buy anything you want, anytime you want it?

As dogs, we know nothing of banks, bills, jobs, or obligations.

My world is one of dreams and full-on joy and happiness every moment of every day.

If I want to play with my toys or sleep for hours, or if I desire to go somewhere (like all over our big yard or exploring new places when we go for our daily car rides we call "Going bye-bye"), I do it and never ask anyone for permission.

I do it because it makes me happy.

You were born to live like that.

To live an unlimited life.

God created everything, and there isn't any dream you can have that will be too big or too much for God to help you have it and live it and love it.

If you always see yourself as a having-bills and barely-getting-by person, that's all you'll ever be.

Let that kind of thinking go.

Start *imagining* yourself and *believing* you *can* live the life you dream of.

Take the limits off the good you allow into your life, and the good that will start to flow into your life will know no limits.

Dear God,

I'm amazed when I look at the vastness and abundance of everything on this earth and know that you created everything and me. I release my old beliefs in lack and limitation and ask for you to replace them with your thoughts of abundance and unlimited possibilities. I'm your child, your creation, and I know deep down inside that what is yours is what can be mine once I believe I can have it and enjoy it. Thank you, God. Yes... Amen.

♥

> ## *If your dream is important to you, you'll find a way, and if it's not, you'll find an excuse"*

The question has been asked, *"Do dogs dream?"*

If you've ever watched us sleep, as we move our legs all over the place and make those funny sounds as we do, it sure makes you think that pup's having a paw-kicking dream.

I go beyond that.

My dream is my desire.

And I always find a way to my desire without stopping for an excuse along the way.

So many of those in your people world can't say that.

You talk a lot about what you're *going* to do, what you'd *like* to do, what you *might* do, and what you *can* do, yet rarely will you say what you *will* do *and then do it.*

You've got a convenient bag of excuses filled with *why not's,* and you just reach down into it and pull one out to give to the world whenever it's *almost* time to take an action to change things in your life.

God has given you dreams, big dreams, and not just to think about.

Those dreams are for you to *have*, to *live*, to *enjoy*, and to *share.*

Those dreams aren't there by mistake.

They're inside of you so you can live them in this life.

So why aren't you living them?

The biggest reason is because you feel unworthy to live them.

They're too big and too grand for you.

Living those dreams would mean leaving the comfortable life you've *struggled* so hard to have, so you could go to something *bigger* and *better*.

What you don't know is that this different life will be filled with far less struggle and far more ease, happiness, and enjoyment.

So you keep yourself from it.

You've reasoned that a life like that is not for you in this lifetime, so you've found some great excuses.

Ones that have been tried and tested on others and that work because you and others believe them.

So here you are.

Living another same old day, just like yesterday and the day before, and not really looking forward to living that same old day tomorrow and in the tomorrows that will follow.

Does that make you happy?

You know it doesn't.

God knows it too.

Try as hard as you may, on this day and all the days you'll be blessed with to live, you'll never feel your greatest joy, happiness, and fulfillment *unless* and *until you live the dreams God has placed inside of you.*

And live by that small voice of the Divine within you that'll always be reminding you…

If your dream is important to you, you'll find a way, and if it's not, you'll find an excuse.

Dear God,

I so want to live the life of my dreams. I let go of the fears and excuses. I let go of living my second, third, or anything less than my favorite choices. In their place, I will live my life of doing only the things I dream and desire to do. Yes, dear God, I can have it all because you created me to do anything I dream of, without limits. Thank you for helping and showing me how to do it. While I may not know everything that's going to happen on the way to my dreams, I don't need to know because I trust you to guide me perfectly to every one of them. You've given me the dreams and desires I have for a reason. It isn't my will, dear God, it's your will be done. Your will is my will because it's always for my divine perfect, and highest, best good and I love knowing that! Everything you do is because of love. Help me to live my life the same way. Thank you. Yes... Amen.

♥

> ## *Plan your dreams on what you want and not on what you have"*

Pretend for a moment you find a book.

This isn't just any old book.

It's a book about how to make *big* things happen in your life.

Inside of it are only a few pages of wisdom and guidance that will take you to anything you want.

You open the book and turn the pages to discover these words…

"Make whatever you want so big that it will excite you…

"Make whatever you want so big that you cannot know all of the steps you will take to achieve it from where you now are…

"Make whatever you want so big that you know you will need others to help you reach it…

"Make whatever you want so big that you don't have anywhere near the money you need to buy it or the knowledge, experience, or money to go right to it and live it…

"Make whatever you want so big that you could not and would not want to have it and achieve it without God as your best friend and partner to go with you to it, every step of the way…

"Now begin it…"

I live that book every day.

I am always reaching for the bigger, the better, the more fun, and the new, and my life is one non-stop blessing after another.

Most of those in your people world can't say that.

They look at where they've been and where they are, and they let those things determine where they're going.

They plan this day and the tomorrows that follow based on what they have and not on what they want.

Imagine if I did that...

Bob and I are in our car going bye-bye (one of our favorite things to do!) and we see a pasture with five cows in it that are standing way off in the distance from where we are.

As quickly as I see those moo-moos (cows), my happy boy barker starts going, my little tail wiggler goes round and round faster than you can count, my eyes open wide and get big as can be, and my paws, legs, and body just can't stop moving!

Just because I see and smell five cows.

What if, after seeing and experiencing the magic of five moo-moos, Bob knows there is another farm just up the road ahead that has fifty moo-moos in it?

Not just fifty moo-moos, but all fifty of them standing near the fence by the road and so close to the road that all we'll need to do is pull our car right next to the fence and I can be standing within *inches* of all fifty of them.

Talk about a Cody dream so big!

So what do you think I would do?

What do you think you would do?

If you're me, your attitude and belief is, *"Bob... I can't believe we're not already there!"*

If you've lived far too many years planning your life based on what you've experienced and what you have in the now, then you may not let yourself go to the unknown where your dream is waiting for you.

What's up ahead is unknown, and things *unknown* create a feeling called *unsure*.

You need to know something.

Where you are and what you have today is only where you are and what you have today.

It's not going be where you can be and go tomorrow.

You didn't get to where you are and what you have right now just by some random chance.

For some time now, you've believed what you're living is what you *should* be living, and all of your beliefs and actions have worked together perfectly to give you everything that matches that belief.

Does your life always have to be like that?

No way!

You can change *any* or *all* of your life to something bigger and better, *anytime* you desire.

You've just got to desire it and have faith and belief in yourself and in God that you will do it.

You will!

Start by doing something as simple as changing *one* of your beliefs.

When you change a belief, you'll also begin to change your actions, which is going to change your results and experiences.

And now you're off to the new life you dream of and desire.

Who knew it could be that easy?

We dogs did.

And now you do too.

Dear God,

I know I can be either the biggest best friend I'll ever have or the toughest critic I'll ever know. It's all my choice. I want to be good to myself again. I want to be happy, really happy, again. I give you everything in my life and ask that you direct every part of it, so that what I think and what I do is in divine perfect harmony with your incredible and amazing plans for me. I bless all of my thinking and beliefs from the past, every single one of them. Thank you for showing me how they helped me to become who I am and have gotten me to the now where I stand. I'm ready to let those old ideas, attitudes, and beliefs go so that the new, fresh, and inspiring ones can now fill my life and help take me to the greatest life you know is possible and you have planned for me. I can do all things through you, dear God, and I so want to and I will. I love you. Thank you. Yes... Amen.

♥

> *Let everything be a possibility just waiting for you to discover"*

Bob and I love spending time around people.

Especially the ones who are happy and have dreams.

As we travel all across the United States and live in so many wonderful states and towns, we notice something interesting…

The happiest people we meet are those, regardless of their age, who look at life believing that everything is a possibility just waiting for them to discover.

And the unhappiest people we meet are those who let their lives be limited, defined and guided by a few unhappy past experiences they've chosen to hold onto and not let go of.

Which of those two groups of people do you resonate with?

I love my life with everything inside of me.

Each day is fresh, vibrant, and new with a clean slate upon which I'm going to write anything my desire calls me to.

And by the end of the night, I will have filled that slate with so many things I enjoyed experiencing and doing that day.

Imagine living your life that way.

Imagine your *only* goal today is to have *fun,* and you're going to fill your day with only the things you want and love to do.

Then you're going to do the same thing tomorrow and the day after and the day after and…

At the end of one week, how different do you think your life would be and feel?

The world is filled with people who are right now living their lives like that.

God created them.

God created you.

So why can't you live your life like that too?

You can!

Everything is a possibility just waiting for you to discover.

Let yourself begin today.

Dear God,

for too long, I've put limits on my life. I've accepted the way others have lived and are living their lives as the way I should do it too. And each time I do so, I feel something deep inside of me saying that's not the way I want to or can live my life. You are calling me forward. You are calling me away from fear, regret, guilt, doubt and worry. You are calling me to follow you to a greater life, a better life, a happier life, and a life filled with possibilities, just waiting for my dreams. You know how I can live it. Take me to it, God. Let's go there together and live it, love it, and enjoy it. You are inspiring me in ways that are thrilling, exhilarating, and astounding. I hear you talking to me. I hear you telling me, "Expect great things, my child. Expect the very best every day and in every way, and you shall have them." I love you God. Thank you. Yes... Amen.

♥

> *When your head says 'No'*
> *and your heart says 'Go,'*
> *listen to the one that'll take*
> *you to where you're best*
> *going to grow"*

The road to your dreams is the most interesting road you'll ever travel.

No one else will ever travel down the same road as you.

Your road is *your* road only, and it will always be *your* road.

People, events, experiences, and lessons are found on your road that won't be found on anyone else's road.

It's all yours.

All along the way on your road that you travel, you'll find learning, growth, and blessings for you alone.

It's all there waiting for you right now.

You need to do just one thing…

Put yourself on your road and start following it.

I love my road.

No other dog that ever lived or will ever live will have my road.

No other dog has my passions and desires and to follow them wherever they may take me.

No other dog has journeyed all over the country like I do with Bob.

No other dog has lived in the same homes and places we have and has had the same experiences in the same ways that Bob and I do.

And no other dog has had or will ever have the love, learning, experiences, and growth that I've had simply by following *my* road.

I listen to God.

I listen to what God is always speaking to me through the desires God gives me.

God has been giving you inspiring desires too, yet you keep ignoring them.

You're fearful of the unknown.

You don't trust yourself to make big changes and to go for a dream of yours that you can't see or know all the steps you'll take before you take even the first step.

You surround yourself with others, *the comfort crowd,* who are afraid just like you, so you can all feel better for not listening to your divine inspirations.

You've become so good at listening to your head that you've forgotten what it feels like to listen to your heart.

It's time for a change.

God has great things waiting for you.

They're all on your road.

God just wants you to get on it.

It's time to let these words be your guiding light…

"When your head says 'No' and your heart says 'Go,' listen to the one that'll take you to where you're best going to grow."

Dear God,

the longer I live, the more I realize how blessed and unique I am. There's no one like me and there never will be. I'm me. You created me to be just who I am. My looks, personality, experiences, and the ways I think and dream and desire are all mine and only mine! I love me! I'm so grateful to you for giving me the gift of life. I love it and I love you, God. From this day on, I want to live my life by my dreams. I want to experience everything in this world by my desires. I want the happy kid inside of me to come out and play and be joyful at all the possibilities that can be mine and are waiting for me to discover, have, love, live, and enjoy. I want all of that and every blessing you have planned for me because everything comes from you, dear God. Everything. You are the reason for me, for us, and for it all. My life is yours. I give you my life and everything in it and ask, with love, trust, and all the faith I have, that you guide my life and make it everything I dream of and everything it can be. Thank you, dear God. I love you, dear God. Thank you. Yes… Amen.

♥

This is only a rest stop on the way to my next stop"

So many times in life, you think you're stuck.

A relationship you got into that's unhappy and isn't working out.

That business deal you hoped would come through that hasn't.

The friend you always thought would be there for you no longer is.

The move you so want to make out of the place you feel stuck in, keeps getting put off.

All of it is enough to zap the joy and excitement right out of you.

Then it happens.

You get a glimmer of hope.

You start thinking differently.

You start thinking, believing, and expecting like me.

You begin looking at life in a fresh new way.

Every delay you're experiencing to the things you want is *just* a delay and *not* a denial.

And every place you've ever been to or lived is just a great place on the way to the next great place.

Then one day it really sinks in…

The place where you now are in your life is not the last stop, but only a rest stop on the way to your next stop.

Now that you know that, I'm giving you a big tail wiggle!

God's calling and desires will never stop at the address you *now* call home.

There's more for you.

So much more just up ahead that God wants to take you to.

Before it can happen, the timing has to be just right.

The place has to be just right.

The people, whom God will put into your life as part of your plan, and you in theirs, have to be just right.

And you have to be *ready* for it to happen.

If there are lessons you still need to learn before God can take you to the next destination, then God will wait until you've learned those lessons before opening the next door.

It's so easy to think that God doesn't care about you when all you've been going through is one delay and frustration after the other.

Yet, God sees the big picture and knows just how it's *all* going to fit together in perfect timing, in the perfect way, and for the blessings and benefit of *all* who are a part of the plan.

That's where faith, trust, and belief come in. God is constantly changing you and doing a good work in and through you *right now*.

Even though it may not seem like it, you have grown so much and in so many ways in just the past year.

You're *so* much further down your life's road than you realize.

And when you're ready—and you soon will be—God will be ready to take you to the *next* incredible blessing and in ways that are going to thrill and amaze you.

Keep your chin up and smile. I've got good news for you.

You are not staying where you are.

It's time to remind yourself...

"This is only a rest stop on the way to my next stop."

Dear God,

I am so grateful to you for being so good to me. You have always taken perfect care of me in every way, and you always will. During those times when I become impatient with myself and others, keep reminding me of how far I've come and how much I've grown. Give me your perspective, dear God, that helps me understand and see the bigger picture of my life, that in one year, two years, five years or however many years from now, so many of the things I'm so focused on right now will be in the rear view mirror and in the past that I've lived, loved, blessed, and let go of. Yes, where I am is not where I'm going or where I'm staying. The new and inspiring are calling me forward and, with you, we're going there together as the best friends who will always be there for each other and loving this life and everything in it with all our heart and soul. I love you so much, God. Thank you. Yes... Amen.

♥

Listen to what's calling your name and go answer its call"

It has the power to keep you awake at night.

It can be the only thing you want to think about.

Yet it doesn't make a sound.

It doesn't need to.

You feel its presence and pull on the inside of you unlike anything else you've ever felt in you life.

It's a calling.

Your calling.

That little tug inside of you that won't let you let go of the dream inside your heart.

The one God placed there a long time ago that hasn't gone anywhere.

The one that goes with you everywhere you go.

Try as hard as you can to not think about it, it won't let you.

It's your passion, your purpose, and your reason for living.

It's where your greatest joy and happiness will be found.

I'm a dog.

I know it.

I listen to it.

I follow it.

I live it.

I love it.

I'm so dialed in and turned on to God that my every thought, action, and experience is filled with divine-soaked joy and happiness and love because *I'm always going where God inspires me.*

Why not you?

You have something that's been calling your name for a long time now.

Something you haven't let yourself follow.

Something you've been too afraid to try.

Something that would *so* change the way you've been living your life that it scares you to think of what a new life could feel and be like.

Something that God wants to take you to.

Something you know God is calling you to.

Your calling.

Trust it.

Trust yourself because you can do it.

This is your time and this is your moment.

Listen to what's calling your name and go answer its call.

Dear God,

I hear you calling me. I feel it inside of me. It's time for me to be taken to my dreams. I want to live, love, and enjoy every one of them, and I ask for your help to show me how. I give you the "Yes" so that you'll take me to the "grow ahead" I'm being called to. I may not know the way, I may not know the when and where, and that's okay with me. I think about the "Why's" of why I want my dreams, and that's going to take me to all of the "How's" I'll ever need for them to happen. You created me to be great, dear God, and you've given me the desires to live, love, and experience greatness. You are incredible. I am incredible. Together we are an unstoppable force of nature. I love you. Thank you. Yes... Amen.

♥

It will never stop whispering to you"

The inspiration from God is one of life's most phenomenal and priceless gifts.

So why don't more of those in your people world follow it?

I *always* do.

I can be sound asleep and suddenly I'll wake up and run to the window to look out or go right to the door and start barking for Bob to let me out.

When he does, I immediately go to a specific place and find exactly what *my inspiration*, the *voice from within*, is telling me to find.

And each and every time Bob is simply amazed to watch it happen.

Just like me, and all of us dogs, you have the *same* divine guidance that's always whispering as the voice inside of you, calling you to a desire that has your name on it.

God is telling you, "Let go of needing to *know* the way before you'll *go* the way."

Your path has already been prepared for you to follow.

So take a few minutes today of quiet time just for you.

Listen to what's whispering your name.

Dear God,

I love knowing that I don't have to know it all or do it all to have the kind of life I dream of. You want to help me. You want to guide me. You want to teach and show me. And you want us to enjoy it all together. From this day on, I will listen to the voice from within, because it is your voice calling me forward to a bigger, better, happier and greater life. Thank you. Yes... Amen.

♥

Run like you've got the wind at your back"

Remember those times in your life when everything you did turned out so easily and so well?

Remember what it felt like when all the people and things that needed to happen just effortlessly and so easily fell into place?

Remember what it felt like when all the compliments and honors for a job well done and a goal well achieved were showered on you?

Remember what it felt like when more money than you ever had was flooding to you, and what it felt like to finally be out of debt and your life awash in the overflow of abundance?

You felt invincible.

You felt untouchable.

You felt immortal.

You felt on top of the world.

You felt like this was only the beginning of the great things about to come your way.

You had the wind at your back, and you soared to heights unimaginable just years earlier.

You'd better get ready.

That wind is coming back.

I love having the wind at my back, and I always know when it's about to happen.

I can *sense* it.

I can *feel* it.

And when it arrives, I run faster than I ever could.

My joy explodes into happiness, as my body and life feel lighter, freer, and able to go anywhere and do anything easier and quicker than before.

That's having the wind at your back.

That's having God take the steering wheel of your life and take you to the next dream and the next dream faster and better than you'll ever be able to do it yourself.

There's something you need to know.

Big changes are on the way to you.

It's time to go to your closet and get out your running shoes.

It's time to dust off your dreams.

With God at your side, you're about to do something again that you love to do...

Run like you've got the wind at your back.

Dear God,

you created me for greatness. I feel it. I know it. And I always have. For so long, I've settled for less than I've wanted and that I'm capable of. I've got such power and potential inside of me that's just been waiting to come out and for me to use it. It's not too late to be what I might have been. I'm ready to be that person now. Thank you for whispering to me, by that voice inside of me that is coming from you, that it's not too late, my time to live my dreams hasn't come and gone, and a fresh, new, and exciting next chapter of my life is waiting for me to live it and love it. I'm ready to run like I've got the wind at my back, and with your guidance and inspiration, I'll always know that wind is coming from you. Thank you. Yes... Amen.

♥

10

YOU ARE AMAZING
AND YOUR LIFE IS
ABOUT TO BECOME
EXTRAORDINARY

> *Everybody wants a new beginning. Here's the good news: You can have it anytime you want."*

The gift of a new day.

Everyone wakes up to it.

So few of you feel blessed by it.

For many, it's just another day to do what they did yesterday and the day before.

For others, this new day is something special.

They're so excited about their lives and what they're doing, that they don't want to go to bed at night and they can't wait to get up in the morning.

The new day called *today* is another chance to learn and grow and get closer to seeing their dreams become a reality.

That's me!

So who are you?

More importantly, who do you *want* to be?

You can have a new beginning at any moment you'd like.

Each day is a new day and a chance to start anew, for life wipes yesterday's slate clean with each new dawn, and Bob and I can't wait to wake up to it.

With God, every second of every day is brand new.

If you feel stuck living your life doing the same old same old and reliving over and over the things from your past, there's good news for you...

God wants to give you a new beginning, starting today.

So how do you start living it?

First, begin *believing* that you *can* live it.

If you can believe it, you can have it.

Next, let God guide you to something new.

That guidance often comes from an inspiration or desire you feel from within.

It can also come from signs from the outside from people you meet and the things they may say and the things you become aware of that seem like a coincidence since they are on the subject of the desire you feel on the inside.

They're not coincidences or random things that just happen.

They're from God, to let you know God hears you and is helping you.

Next, get out of your own way.

One of the biggest obstacles those in your people world create that keeps God from doing all the good that God wants to do in your lives, is by thinking you know better than God, what you need and how it should come to you.

If you were so good at that, you'd already have it, be living it, and be enjoying it.

Let go of the steering wheel and let God get behind the wheel and take you to where you next want to go.

Be more like me and be the passenger as you enjoy the amazing and thrilling ride!

You can't stick your head out of every window in the car and feel the excitement and the wind in your face as you see all the sights, smell all the smells, and hear all the sounds as you're going down the road, if you always think you've got to be behind the wheel as the driver.

Let God do the driving and take you to all the new beginnings in your life that are just up ahead.

Dear God,

I love new beginnings. I love knowing my past is not my future and I can begin again every day and in every way. Help me to know what I want and why I really want it. In this world of so much information, so much noise and distraction all trying to get my attention, keep my connection to you open and flowing and always on. Never stop talking to me, guiding me, helping me, taking care of me, inspiring me, blessing me, and loving me. I let go of what was, so you will always have room in my life to bring me what is and what will be. I love you, dear God. Thank you. Yes... Amen.

♥

You've come much further than you think"

It's so easy to think not much has changed in your life.

So many of you in your people world find yourselves in a rut from time to time.

You keep thinking that little to nothing is different in your lives.

Yet, look back to a year ago.

Look at how *much* you've changed.

You *now* think differently about things.

You *now* act differently about things.

You *now* understand and *know* differently about things.

Many of the things that once interested you or you thought were important, no longer are, or at least not the way they used to be.

They've now been replaced by new beliefs, new interests, and different things that are important to who you are *today*.

The power of a dog can be a powerful reminder of that.

That's one of the things I love to do for Bob.

I do that by living our life's journey together as best friends.

All the places we've been and all the places we're going have been priceless for our growth, joy, and happiness.

It's one of life's greatest gifts and most beautiful experiences.

And here's one of the reasons why…

With each new state and town we move to, it's as if we arrive there to a brand new, unwritten chalkboard just waiting for us to write on it.

To be written with all the things we'll do, where we'll go, whom we'll meet, and what we'll learn together.

And we do.

At the end of each year, we love looking back on our time and the experiences we've had traveling and living in that location.

Bob loves talking to me about the things we did and are doing there.

I just love hearing Bob talk to me about our life together, and Bob does too.

Just writing down or talking about what happened and is happening in our lives is always such a powerful reminder of how far God has brought us, and what incredible possibilities for a bigger and better life are waiting for us, just up ahead.

It can be the same for you.

So let's get your life moving in a great new direction.

Grab a pen and paper.

Write down as many things you can think of that happened to you in just the last year.

Pick out the experiences you planned and those you didn't plan, and make a few notes about what you learned from each of them.

Now, on a clean sheet of paper, write down five things (or more) you'd like to have happen in the next 12 months.

Then write down *why* you'd like them to happen.

Write down how it will make you feel once those "on the way to me" things *become* your reality.

Each week, look at that "What I'd Like to Have Happen" list and let it become a part of your weekly, then daily, routine.

Now watch how your life begins to change.

Your life is supposed to be happy, fun, and filled with joy.

Starting right now, be easier and less critical and demanding on yourself.

Each day, stop for a moment and give yourself a big hug.

You're doing great, and everything is only going to get better.

A lot better.

Always remember where you were before you got to where you are.

With each new day, you're going to realize you've come so much further than you thought.

And just wait until you see what's up ahead waiting for you!

It will be amazing.

Yes, *you* are amazing!

Dear God,

so many times I think I'm not getting anywhere and so little in my life ever seems to change. Yet, as I look at where I am now and back at where I've been, it amazes me to realize that so much in my life has changed. I'm not the same person I was ten years ago, and I'll not be the same person ten years from now that I am today. God, I know you've been with me the whole time and you've never left me. You've always been by my side and, whether I realized it at the time or not, you've always been guiding, helping, protecting, and blessing me. I am so grateful and thankful for this and for you. Help me to enjoy this day and all the moments in it, for I am thankful for them all. Help me to start dreaming big things and new ideas again. Show me and inspire me that the rest of my life will be the best of my life. I put everything in it, and everything I am and will ever be, in your hands, dear God. I love you. Thank you. Yes... Amen.

♥

> *Inside of you right now is the power that will change your life. One day you will decide to use it. How about today?"*

Those in your people world will search for many years of their lives for secrets, tips, information, knowledge, and advice.

They'll search for anything that can bring them more happiness, success, money, and the good life.

They'll read books, attend seminars by experts, watch videos, and listen to audios by those who seemingly have the answers to the missing piece they seek.

Then one day, it hits them.

After all the years of time and money spent, they look at their lives and only rarely find that where they are matches up to where they want and hope to be.

The day that begins to change is when they realize where the answer can be found to whatever they desire…

Inside of them.

I came to this earth knowing from the first day of my first breath where anything and everything I could ever want, dream of or desire would be found.

Inside of me.

Like you, Bob, me, and everyone else, I came to this earth connected to my creator.

The difference is, I've never let go of that connection in search of a better one.

Especially from those who proclaim they know better than we how to live our lives.

Inside of you is the power that will change your life to anything you can ever hope or dream it can be.

Anything.

That power is given to you by God.

Yet power is only *potential* power unless and until it is used.

It cannot do anything for you until the day and moment comes that you acknowledge it, and then use it, for the good life God is inspiring you to have and to live.

I use my power every moment of every day, and my life is extraordinary.

It is time for yours to be too.

Dear God,

I've always known there's something inside of me that's bigger than I've ever known. Bigger and greater than I've ever let myself experience. Bigger and far more phenomenal than I've ever let myself become. That power is you, living inside of me. A power so great that it can change my life for the best in the blink of an eye and can help me inspire something in others that can change their lives just as dramatically and wonderfully. Help me to bring it out, dear God. Help me to know it and to use it only for love and blessings and for my own and others' divine best good. Help me to use every bit of it to so I can do your will and keep doing your will for as long as you will bless me with this gift of my life. I'm here to make a difference and to help others. You're my best friend. I love you. Let's change people's lives and our world and do amazing things together. I love you, dear God. Thank you so much. Yes... Amen.

♥

Find your rock and stand on it"

When Bob and I moved to the New York City area, we were thrilled at all the undiscovered possibilities and adventures that awaited us.

Upon our arrival, one of the first things we did was go to the ocean.

When we arrived at Westhampton Beach and saw and heard the ocean there for the first time, we were excited beyond words!

As soon as my paws touched the sand, off I flew, as I'd run up and down the beach and out into the surf and back, again and again.

I was having the time of my life!

It was non-stop excitement, as I sniffed, tail wiggled, and ran my legs as fast as I could, soaking in every new and exciting thing I smelled, tasted, touched, and saw.

And you should've seen Bob!

He just laughed and loved watching me play and frolic and be so happy and filled with so much joy.

I just loved watching Bob laugh and smile and giggle at how wonderful it felt to be together at one of our most favorite places in the world—at the ocean.

After running up and down the beach and in and out of the ocean, I found a huge group of rocks that were stretched out from the shore all the way into the ocean.

And what did I do when I saw them?

Find my favorite rock, climb up on it and stand on it.

Just like I was Cody, the King of the Ocean!

As I stood on my rock and the ocean waves crashed up against the rock all around me, I just kept looking at Bob and thinking about *him*.

I didn't care about what was behind me or around me.

All I cared and thought about was Bob, and I was unmovable.

I was *on my rock.*

Just loving this life and Bob's life, and thankful to God for this moment to know what love feels like and is lived like.

Just what God wants you to experience and enjoy.

And it's easier than you may think.

When your thoughts stay on God, you are *always* on your rock.

You're unmovable and unshakable.

In life, there may be times when it feels like the waves of the things you're thinking about and dealing with are crashing all around you.

Times when it seems like any wave of good news, good breaks, opportunities, happiness and joy have gone far out to sea without a hint of their return.

Just hold on.

Keep standing on your rock.

Every crashing wave *always* disappears.

And when it does, watch how quickly the waves of abundance, good news, and blessings come right in for you.

When your faith, belief, and trust are in God, you're standing on your rock.

You're looking ahead at the God who is always looking ahead and holding onto and looking after you.

Always and eternally.

So start walking. There it is.

Bob and I can see it just up ahead.

It's your rock. It's time for you to stand on it.

Dear God,

in this life, it's easy to get caught up in the things happening in my life and in others' lives too. Before I realize it, my thoughts and feelings can go off in so many directions. Places where it feels like I'm miles down the road and so far away from the happy place where I was, that at times I can feel a bit lost and unsure of how to quickly get back to where I want to be again. I know I want to be on my rock. To be steady, sure, knowing, secure, and ready to do the things I want to do and follow the dreams I so want to experience. God, I ask that you put me on my rock and keep me on it wherever I go, whatever I think, and whatever I do. I know you are always with me, in me, standing before, behind, and beside me. I know that whenever I feel unsure and my footing and life start to feel a bit shaky, you will always be there holding me, helping me, and never letting me go. You are my best friend, God. I love you. I thank you. Use me to do your will. I'm here for you and for others. You created me to live this life and to love every moment of it. With the gifts, talents, and abilities that you've so lovingly blessed me with, I want us to do amazing things and touch people's lives for the best in any ways we can. I'm ready. I'm unstoppable. I'm yours. Thank you. Yes… Amen.

♥

Every street has our name on it"

You come into this world preloaded with possibilities.

So many of you leave it overloaded with problems.

So what happened to you along the way?

We dogs know.

You listened to others instead of listening and following the guidance of God from within.

Those in your people world make life so much harder than it ever needs to be.

The desire to fit in and be accepted can be so great that before you realize it, you've let yourself change identities from *who you really are, to who you hope they'll see you to be.*

I love inspiring Bob by showing him I never accept anyone else's expectation of whom I should be, what I should do, what I should have, and what I can experience.

For me, everything everywhere is a possibility that waits only for my exploration of it.

Bob will be the first to tell you what a blessing that is for him to watch and experience each day.

Bob and I have become so good at living our lives without limits, that it would feel so unlike us to live them any other way.

Take living in places where the wealthy live.

Places where the homes are astounding and the beliefs by those who enjoy them know few limits.

Bob and I love to spend time driving around these areas because it's just so inspiring.

We know that we too belong there.

There's never any of this *"These homes look expensive, Bob, are you sure we should be going down this street?"* from me.

Or Bob.

We know we are kings.

We know we are God's.

We know we deserve it.

God has taught us, through the thoughts we think and the inspiration we feel, that God knows no limits to what God can do in our lives except those we place on ourselves by what we believe we are worthy to live, to have, and to enjoy.

God is always calling us higher, to be more, to experience more, and to be better and greater than we are.

And we love answering the call.

Whenever Bob and I squeeze all the juice out of each place where we're living and God is calling us to the *next* great place and experience, that divine voice inside of us lets us know…

"This place feels small. Let's go someplace bigger and better that'll inspire us more."

So few of you in your people world will let God speak to you in ways that'll move you—*on both the inside and the outside.*

You deny yourself the things you truly want when you never need to.

It's time for things to be different.

Bob and I have a message for you…

"If what you're doing makes you unhappy, *change.*"

"If where you live doesn't inspire you, *move.*"

"If you don't enjoy those you hang out with, *let them go.*"

You won't get any rewards, *either in the here or in the after,* by keeping from yourself the things God wants to give to you.

Reconnect with your creator and talk to God again.

Listen to your guidance from within.

You will always receive it.

Follow that guidance and then tell no one.

What you're supposed to do is just between God and you.

Once you arrive at the next great place God wants to take you, all the right people, at just the right times, are going to show up in your life.

Nothing in this life is by randomness, coincidence, or chance.

You are being *guided.*

You are being *helped.*

You are being *protected.*

You are being *blessed.*

You are a divine masterpiece.

You are God's divine child.

You are a king.

You are a queen.

And every street has your name on it.

Dear God,

with every fiber of my being I know I am great. I know I was born to be great. I know I can be great from this day and this moment on. Thank you for creating inside me the desire to know it, to feel it, to release it, and to be it. As I look around at those in this life who've achieved incredible things and enjoy the things I too desire to have and experience, I ask myself, "if they can have it, why can't I?" They are your children. I am your child. And if some of your children can be mightily blessed, then all of your children can be mightily blessed. From this day and moment on, I want you to be my best friend. I want you to take and guide everything in my life and show me the way, so I can know, be, and do everything you've called and created me to do on this earth. You gave me life for a mighty purpose. You provide for and take perfect care of me because you love me and need me to help you so we can bless others. There is nothing too great for us to do. There is nothing too much for us to have. There is nothing too spectacular that I cannot become. There is no goal or dream too big for us to enjoy. And there is never too much love that I can feel and give to myself and to everyone I meet. We will change the world. And we're going to do it together. You, as my God and creator. And I, as your child who loves you with all of my heart and soul forever. I love you, dear God. I thank you, dear God. Yes… Amen.

♥

Thank you for reading our book!

We'd love to hear your story
of how our words and inspirations
have touched your life at
CodyandBob.com.

With Love and Blessings to you,
Bob & Cody

Facebook: /codyandbobinspires
Instagram: @codyandbob

Words That Inspired Me

Words That Inspired Me

Words That Inspired Me

Words That Inspired Me

Words That Inspired Me

Words That Inspired Me

Words That Inspired Me

Words That Inspired Me

Words That Inspired Me

Made in United States
Troutdale, OR
06/05/2023

10451877R00160